The Root Cause Analysis Handbook

ROOT CAUSE ANALYSIS

A Simplified Approach to Identifying, Correcting, and Reporting Workplace Errors

MAX AMMERMAN

PRODUCTIVITY
productivity press

Printed in the United States of America
Productivity Press
444 Park Avenue South, Suite 604
New York, NY 1016
United States of America
Telephone: 212-686-5900
Telefax: 212-686-5411
E-mail: info@productivitypress.com

Library of Congress Cataloging-in-Publication Data

Ammerman, Max.
  The root cause analysis handbook : a simplified approach to identifying,correcting, and reporting workplace errors / Max Ammerman.
     p.   cm.
  ISBN 0-527-76326-8 (alk. paper)
   1. Quality control—Data processing.   2. Industrial accidents—Investigation.
3. Problem solving.   I. Title.
TS156.A46   1997
658.5—dc21   9734888
                                                                 CIP

05   7 6

Contents

Introduction

Overview of Chapters

Process Steps	Comments
Significant Event Occurs (notified to evaluate)	The Introduction will cover the relationship of this methodology to evaluating events or other performance problems.
↓	
Define Problem/ Collect Initial Data (Chapter 1)	This section is important to ensure that the focus of your (the team's) work is kept on correcting the initial problem. Collecting data will start here and continue throughout the process.
↓	
Perform Task Analysis (Chapter 2)	This step is important to identify any conditions that may contribute to the performance of the task.
↓	
Perform Change Analysis (Chapter 3)	This step will examine the task in depth. This is most important when you (the team) seem "stuck."
↓	
Perform Control Barrier Analysis (Chapter 4)	This step is the first tool that identifies potential causes. Many simple problems can be evaluated using this tool.
↓	
Begin Event Causal Factor Chart (Chapter 5)	This tool integrates the whole event. When complete it tells what happened, explains why it happened, and shows the barriers to improve.
↓	
Conduct Interviews (Chapter 6)	This is the most important step in the evaluation process. This is where you (the team) get the information necessary to solve the "problem."

1

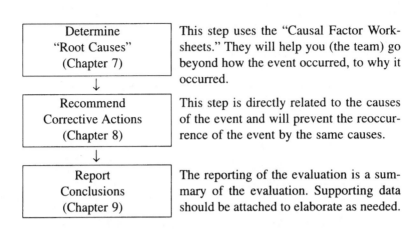

Determine "Root Causes" (Chapter 7)	This step uses the "Causal Factor Work-sheets." They will help you (the team) go beyond how the event occurred, to why it occurred.
Recommend Corrective Actions (Chapter 8)	This step is directly related to the causes of the event and will prevent the reoccur-rence of the event by the same causes.
Report Conclusions (Chapter 9)	The reporting of the evaluation is a sum-mary of the evaluation. Supporting data should be attached to elaborate as needed.

Background

This book presents tools and methods to evaluate "significant events." The same tools can be used to evaluate any *event, near miss,* or *potential problem.* The tools originated in the Human Performance Enhancement System (HPES) used by nuclear power stations throughout the United States. Florida Power & Light Company (FPL) incorporated these tools in the Problem Identification and Correction (PIC) classes taught to management to improve human reliability in their areas. Thus, the book uses the acronym PIC to refer to the process.

This method is used to perform "single case boring." The process allows the determination of causes for a single event. This is important when a reoccurrence of the event is not acceptable. When previous classes (i.e., quality improvement classes) directed "single case boring," to be performed but did not explain how to do it, this is it. During FPL's "Deming Challenge," this method was used to improve the human side of the equation and, in general, any performance problem.

This method to evaluate events is used to evaluate any undesirable event. This is particularly true if the event involves "human error." However, the method may also be used for equipment problems. This can be work related or any event. The real question becomes economics. If the consequence is not significant, don't spend much effort trying to fix the cause.

Terms

There is a glossary at the end of this handbook. Generally, the first or second time a unique word is used, it will be in italics, indicating that the word is included in the glossary.

The word *you* will refer to you—the evaluator—or to you—the team—whichever is appropriate.

Subject Matter/Chapters of Handbook

The steps described in this text are in the sequence in which they should be performed, and will lead you through the process to determine what happened, how it happened, and why it happened. Based on the *causes* of the *event, corrective actions* will be implemented to prevent reoccurrence. The steps (sections of the handbook) are as follows:

Chapter 1: Define Problem

This chapter will introduce the problem you are evaluating and will help maintain the focus of the evaluation throughout the process. Many times, while evaluating an event, there are problems that are identified that are not directly related to the cause of the initial problem. It is very easy to get sidetracked on these other issues and waste valuable time. It's not that these other issues are not important, but they deserve a separate evaluation. This is also the step where initial information is collected. This data will help define the problem and present a starting point for the evaluation. This short duration step is important, especially in serious events.

Chapter 2: Task Analysis

This chapter is for the evaluator who is not a "subject matter expert." This step will give insight into the task and produce the questions that will guide the interviews. A task analysis will take only a short time, but will be essential to a thorough evaluation.

Chapter 3: Change Analysis

This chapter is for an in-depth understanding of this particular task. It presents the tool to use when you are stumped. When you have interviewed and have constructed an Event and Causal Factor Chart (ECFC), and the inappropriate actions and causes are not apparent, this is the most important time to perform a task analysis.

Chapter 4: Control Barrier Analysis

This is the first tool that looks at possible causes of an event. These causes would initially be *potential causes* that need validation during the evaluation. In many simple events, this tool may be the only one necessary to use.

Chapter 5: Event and Causal Factor Chart

This is the most powerful tool presented and is used in most (>95%) event evaluations. (An ECFC was a tool used to evaluate the Challenger disaster.) This tool presents the "big picture" of the event. It shows what happened, how it happened, and why it happened. The ECFC also incorporates control barrier analysis and change analysis. The only items missing on this chart are the corrective actions to prevent reoccurrence of the event.

Chapter 6: Interviews

Interviews are the single most important method used to evaluate any event. This is the step that gathers quantities of data to analyze. This data identifies potential causes and verifies root causes and contributing causes. This information fills in the details of the ECFC. Interviewing is the most important step in the evaluation.

Interviewing is much more than just asking someone questions. When done properly, the interviews are very focused. They feed directly into the ECFC. Your questions should: 1) fill in the holes in the ECFC, and 2) verify data as necessary. The answers you receive should immediately be incorporated into the ECFC. The ECFC prepares you for the next interview. Toward the end of an evaluation, you already know the answers. You are only verifying data and ensuring you did not overlook any areas. The structure of interviewing is covered thoroughly in this chapter.

Chapter 7: Root Causes

"Root causes" is a slight misnomer. These are actually called causal factors. The causal factors may be classified as "root" causes, contributing causes, and possible causes. This chapter will allow you to identify the causal factors of the event and "weigh" each into the correct classification.

The causal factor worksheets will be an invaluable aid to identify the causes of the event. There are other uses for these worksheets that are discussed in this chapter.

Chapter 8: Corrective Actions

This includes more than corrective actions. This chapter will define and discuss corrective, mitigating, and adaptive actions. These are derived from the ECFC and the barrier analysis. The countermeasures matrix is one method used to select the appropriate actions. Sometimes, it is not feasible to correct all the causal factors. Occasionally, even a "root" cause may not be feasible to correct. Selecting the appropriate actions (recommendations) is not always straightforward. These considerations will be discussed.

Chapter 9: Report

The report is the most visible document you will compose. It must present and summarize your evaluation. The most efficient format is as follows: 1) define the problem, 2) what happened/event summary, 3) why it happened/cause of the event, 4) corrective actions/recommendations.

Format

At certain points, there will be an area that will include (as appropriate for the particular section):

- **Hints**—good things to do or reference. They will make your evaluation easier to do.
- **Shortcuts**—good things to do or reference. They will make your evaluation faster.
- **Pitfalls** to avoid. As you start a new step, it helps to be reminded what doesn't work.

Comments

The handbook is written as an informal document. We hope it will avoid the stiffness of a technical manual and be more like a coaching instrument. The material is presented in the same order that it is performed. Each section includes an example that will jog your memory as to the end product. When evaluating events, in the future, you may find it helpful to refer to the examples in the handbook.

This method of evaluation is to be used as a basic guide. These are proven tools, but, in the course of the evaluation, if other tools and assistance are necessary, use other tools or request assistance through your management chain. You should use these tools to evaluate the event, but you are not limited to only these tools (see Appendix: Other Root Cause Analysis Tools).

In conclusion, it is essential first to understand what happened before attempting to understand the causes. Once you understand the mechanism(s) that existed during the equipment or human performance event, then you can determine why the behavior or failure occurred (causes) and what causal factors contributed to the problem. Once you know the cause(s), you can determine the best corrective action(s) to implement. This process—applicable to equipment failures, design problems, and human performance problems—is not complete until you communicate your results to management and others involved in implementing the corrective action and review the effectiveness of your corrective action(s).

When time is short and data is not readily available, it is tempting to look only at the symptoms of problems and take actions as quickly as possible to attempt to fix the symptom. To completely identify and correct a problem, you need a methodology or process to guide you in conducting a complete investigation to ensure problems are eliminated and prevented from recurring. The PIC method provides such a framework.

Scenario for Examples in Handbook

Scenario: Misposition of Switch 8G 176—Initial Information

Background

At electrical power plants, the electricity is generated and connects to the system grid through a switch yard. In the switch yard, the high voltage electricity is directed by large switches to the desired output line. In this event, one of the high voltage lines will be worked on in December at approximately 0800 (8:00 A.M.).

To maintain the line de-energized, the utility uses a switching order. This is a formal work control to take the line out of service and keep it isolated during the work. The switching order directs the operation of the large switches and directs the placement of (red danger) hold tags to prevent the inadvertent operation of the switches.

The Event

On the morning of December 28, 1995, at 0655, the dispatcher (a utility employee that controls the production and distribution of electricity) calls the XYZ power plant to execute a switching order. The switching order is to support work on a high voltage line. That work is scheduled to start at 0800. The operator (switchman) writes the switching order and reads it back. He is given a start time of 0700.

The switchman enters the switch yard with an operator trainee and executes the switching order. The trainee watches as he calls back the dispatcher and reports the switching order complete at 0720. The switchman and trainee are relieved at 0730 and go home.

The line crew arrives at work location and fuzzes (checks to see if the line is energized) the line. The line is energized. The dispatcher is notified, and the switch positions are checked by a day shift switchman at the XYZ power plant. Contrary to the danger tag, switch 8G 176 is found closed and the motor engaged. The dispatcher is informed, and a new switching order is executed to allow the line work to begin.

Due to the potential seriousness of this event and other switching problems that had recently occurred, a team is formed to review this event. You are called at the office to join the team to determine the cause of this event and make recommendations to prevent similar occurrences in the future.

As the team arrives at the plant, they have the original switching order that was executed at 0720. They have a statement made by the switchman that checked the switch position at 0810. He states that he entered the switch yard at 0805 and found switch 8G 176 closed and the motor engaged. He and the dispatcher corrected the problem with a new switching order.

Day Shift
Switchman's Statement

I took the shift at 0730. At 0805, a call was received from the dispatcher to check the position of 8G 176. I entered the switch yard at 0810 and found a danger tag on 8G 176 to maintain it in the open position with the motor disengaged. However, 8G 176 was shut and the motor was engaged.

There was a crew of contractors in the switch yard. I could not tell what they were doing, and I did not see anyone else in the yard.

I called the switch position into the dispatcher and he gave me a new switching order to open 8G 176. I opened the switch and disengaged the motor. A new danger tag was hung.

SWITCHING ORDER

John Dunn   No. *1234*
SWITCHMAN

At *Vila*   - *472*   Date *12-28* 19 *95*
STATION   NUMBER

IMPORTANT - READ THESE INSTRUCTIONS FIRST

A. As each step is executed **VISUALLY VERIFY** proper position of switch blades, semaphores and motor operators.
B. Execute in the **EXACT SEQUENCE GIVEN**.
C. If **ANY DISCREPANCY** is noted, **STOP IMMEDIATELY AND REPORT TO THE DISPATCHER**.

STEP NO.		Completed & Visually Verified	TIME
1	Verify station No. with dispatcher and enter No. (*472*)	x	0700
2	OP 8 W 134	x	0711
3	OP 8 W 129	x	0712
4	OP 8 G 176	x	0713
5	Disengage motor & tag 8 G 176	x	0713
6	CI 8 W 129	x	0714
7	CI 8 W 134	x	0715

Given By _____*Jones*_____   *0700* A.M *12-28*19*95*
               DISPATCHER   P.M..

Executed By ___*J Dunn*___   *0720* A.M *12-28*19*95*
                  SWITCHMAN   P.M..

Reported Executed To ___*Jones*___   *0721* A.M *12-28*19*95*
                            DISPATCHER   P.M..

Reported to _____   ___ A.M _____ 19__
          (LOAD) (DISTRIBUTION) DISPATCHER   P.M..

Clearance No. ___*Smith 496*___

Form 970 (Stocked) Rev 1/79

Figure 1. Scenario: original switching order.

1

Define Problem/ Collect Data

There are two parts to this "first" step. In order to define the problem, you must have some initial information. Therefore, collecting data is also part of this first step. When you start your evaluation, gather all the available initial information, then define the problem. Throughout the evaluation, additional data is gathered.

Since the purpose of this chapter is to define the problem, we will cover this part first. The second part of Chapter 1 covers collecting data that will be used through the rest of the evaluation.

Define the Problem

What Is the Purpose of Defining the Problem?

The purpose of this first step in the PIC process is to clearly and specifically identify and describe the problem you are trying to solve in an effort to focus your root cause analysis and corrective action efforts. You must identify what, who, when, where, and how about the undesirable situation in order to clearly define the problem. During your systematic efforts to define the problem, you may also reveal multiple problems that you should handle separately.

What Is a "Problem"?

A problem is:

— a deviation from a requirement or expectation;

— when "actual" is different from "should";

— an undesirable event, situation, or performance trend; and/or

— the primary effect critical for a situation to occur.

In most cases, identifying "what the problem is" is easy. If you are on a significant event evaluation, you were told the "problem" when you were summoned to join the team. The management team may have assigned you a problem to solve. You may have observed an event, a near miss, or a negative trend. These will be cues to "what the problem is." It is still up to you to define the problem.

Why Is It Important to Define the Problem?

Clearly stating the problem is a key to problem identification and correction. You must define the undesirable event or problem situation so that everyone involved in its solution understands it. A clearly defined problem focuses your investigative efforts and saves time. Finally, honest effort at careful definition will avoid the "ready, fire, aim" approach that is so common in problem-solving. A problem that is not properly defined may result in failure to reach the proper resolution.

When to Define the Problem

In your first step of the evaluation, as you gather your initial information, define the problem. When an undesirable event occurs, you may face only suspected problem areas and/or conditions that are not well defined or substantiated by facts. In addition, the manner in which the problem is described for you initially may be very subjective, opinionated, or ambiguous. Therefore, you need a well-defined problem (undesirable event/primary effect) to focus the scope of your root cause analysis and solution selection. Sometimes, as the evaluation progresses, you find additional information that may require that the problem be redefined.

Criteria for a Well-Defined Problem

1. It focuses on the gap. The gap between what is and what should be reflects a change or deviation from the requirement, norm, standard, or expectation.
2. It states the effect. It states what is wrong, not why it is wrong.

The following are other characteristics of a well-defined problem:

- It is measurable. It says how often, how much, when. It avoids broad and ambiguous categories like "morale," "productivity," "communication."
- It is stated in a positive manner and describes the pain, e.g., the valve leaks.

- It avoids "lack of" and "no" statements. These imply solutions. For example, "lack of food" or "no food" implies food as the solution, while the problem is hunger.
- It highlights the significance of effects. It may state areas of discomfort, hurt, or annoyance, or how people are affected.

You may need two simple statements to accomplish all of the above. The following are example statements that represent well-defined problems:

- The overflow valve has activated four times within ten days, posing a threat to equipment and personnel safety.
- The auxiliary equipment operator spilled ten gallons of sulfuric acid on the cement pad of the water treatment plant while performing a regeneration. This action violated EPA requirements and necessitated a report to environmental regulators.
- Over the past three weeks, 83 work orders were returned to the Maintenance Department for required signatures resulting in a 30% increase in processing time.

All of these statements focus on the gap between "what is happening" and "what should be happening," and are measurable, specific statements that have no implied solutions. All of them state what is wrong—the effect(s) that result from a deviation. They do not include any "why," "lack of," or "due to" elements.

Finding the "why," the "due to," and the "lack of" is all part of root cause analysis. To speculate with little data and no idea of the cause–effect relationship between the sequence of events and contributing factors that led to the gap would be a waste of time without a well-defined problem.

How to Define the Problem

Organize the initial information you have around what, who, when, where, how much, and how many. See Table 1-1 for questions you might use to organize your data. Next, assess the magnitude of the problematic situation, and determine if immediate action is required to prevent the situation from getting worse. Identify any additional information you need to clearly define the problem so you can focus your root cause analysis efforts. Finally, determine what data you will collect and which tools you will use to proceed.

Collect Data

Collection of data addresses the what, who, where, when, how much, and how many questions. To collect your data, use the following tools to identify and define the problem. In addition to the questions presented in Table 1-1, the tools that help organize data about a problem situation are the event sequence/timeline and the situational analysis forms.

These are described followed by a discussion.

TABLE 1-1.

Descriptive Facts About the Problem

CATEGORY	QUESTIONS
What	1. What equipment, machine, or tool 2. What is wrong, what is the complaint 3. What undesired behavior is involved
Who	1. Which individual(s) are involved: employees, internal staff, customers, clients, suppliers, bystanders—by name and/or position
When	1. When does it occur: day, date, time 2. What shift or phase of operation 3. During what part of plant/equipment life cycles 4. What time pattern is involved
Where	1. Which unit, area, department 2. Location of defective item or defect on item
How	1. How is the "what" or "who" affected 2. Injury, death, shutdown, trip, startup, damage, type, or classification of defect
How Much How Many	1. Quarterly affected components or persons 2. How many times affected; how much of item affected; how many defects per item

Event Sequence/Timeline

It is important to begin developing an event sequence as soon as you've been notified of the event. You can create a timeline on your wall or whiteboard with self-stick removable notes, or use a computer. As you collect and analyze additional information, you have a baseline of facts to return to keep your focus. This sequence will be used to begin the Event and Causal Factor Chart (see Chapter 5). Depending on the problem, you may choose to sketch a diagram showing a piece of equipment or process flowchart in addition to or instead of an event sequence.

Hint: When writing down your event sequence/timeline, make a note of where that piece of information came from. In very significant events, you may be questioned as to "how you know that." Keep the source of your information linked to each fact.

Considerations for Collecting Data

Assess the magnitude of the situation. Ask yourself the following:

- Is this a recurring problem?
- Is the root cause difficult to find?
- Is the situation critical?
- Is the situation likely to get worse if no action is taken?
- Is there a potential for other problems to develop while you are investigating this situation?
- Is this item getting high management or regulatory attention?
- Where is the deviation from requirements?
- Are there several deviations from requirements?
- What resources will you need to evaluate, analyze, and resolve the problem(s)?

How to Collect Data

Data collection is performed throughout the evaluation process. Therefore, several of the following methods of collecting data will simply refer you to the appropriate section in the manual.

Decide How to Record Data

Problem solvers often have trouble recording data so that it is easily retrievable and useful later. You can use any of several techniques to record data, for example:

- Worksheet/chart
- Card
- Log

You should use the recording technique that fits your situation, your collection method, and your own preferences.

Ways You Might Collect Data

- Review records, logs, or videotapes.
- Conduct interviews with personnel involved in the event.

- Conduct interviews with subject matter experts regarding possible consequences of corrective actions.
- Ask for written statements (when interviewing is not possible) using a form such as the one in Significant Event Evaluation, Initial Data Gathering Forms (Appendix A).
- Observe the actual scene of the event (ASAP).
- Take photographs of or sketch equipment, facility, or process layout.
- Observe the effects of corrective action(s).
- Perform or request laboratory tests.
- Perform the work tasks you are investigating yourself.

Next are guidelines and techniques for using each of the four common data collection methods.

Reviewing Documents

1. Review relevant documents or portions of documents as necessary and reference their use. Record appropriate dates and times associated with the event/problem on the documents reviewed. Following is a sample list of documents:

   Operating/working logs

   Correspondence

   Meeting minutes

   Inspection/testing records

   Maintenance records

   Equipment history records

   Computer records

   Recorder tracings

   Procedures and/or instructions

   Vendors manuals

   Drawings and specifications

   Design information

   Change documents

   Trend charts and graphs

   Plant parameter readings

   Sample analysis and results

2. Review equipment supplier and manufacturer records for correspondence addressing the problem(s).

Conducting Observations (at the Workplace)

This method is like a walk-through task analysis, which is covered in detail in Chapter 2.

Conducting Surveys

A survey is one method that can verify impressions you received during the evaluation. This method allows you to collect data from a large group of people. It is not often used during the problem identification and correction process. If you need to develop, implement, and analyze the results of a survey, you should seek the help of someone experienced in the use of this tool.

Interviews

This is covered in detail in Chapter 6.

Data Collection Guidelines

You may need to make requests for data or obtain permission to interview people or review records in advance. You may need to explain why you need the information you are requesting and how you will use it.

The following are a few general guidelines for collecting data:

- Collect data pertinent to conditions:

    before, during, and after the event

    environmental factors such as weather conditions

    time of day, day of the week, amount of overtime worked.
- When taking a series of photographs, carefully document and label each photograph (e.g., keep a note or log showing pertinent information—sequence of photographs, distances, orientations, times, etc.).
- Collect, label, and preserve physical evidence such as:

    failed components

    ruptured gaskets

    burned leads

    blown fuses

    spilled fluids

    partially completed work orders or procedures
- Establish a quarantine area for failed equipment or components, or tag and separate pieces and material. It is important to do these things despite operational pressures to restore equipment to service.

- Consider things that occurred around the event area that seem, at first, to be nonrelevant. For example:

  hardware (equipment) or software (programmatic-type issues) associated with the event

  recent program or equipment changes

  physical environment (location)

- Review and verify the data to ensure accuracy and objectivity. Ask yourself questions such as:

  Is eyewitness testimony consistent?

  Does the information support the physical evidence?

  Is more information needed? (Focus on the key issues.)

  Do I need to hold a second interview to check certain aspects of the situation?

  Has information been used in such a way as to overcome personal bias?

Pitfalls of Data Collection

The data collection process has several pitfalls:

- Information can become lost or distorted.
- Information can be incomplete.
- You can waste time collecting too much data.

How to Overcome the Pitfalls of Lost or Distorted Data

1. Understand the ways that information and data can become lost or distorted. The various ways that this can occur include:

   Loss of information

   People: forget

   overlook

   neglect to record information

   do not want to get involved

   Physical: taken

   misplaced

   cleaned up

   destroyed

   taken apart or repaired

   conditions lost

Paper: overlooked

misplaced

taken

destroyed

Distortion of information

People: remember incorrectly

rationalize

misrepresent

misunderstand

perceive differently

feel stress differently

Physical: moved

altered

disfigured

supplemented

Paper: altered

disfigured

misinterpreted

2. Use techniques to avoid loss or distortion of information:

(**Hint:** Before an event occurs, establish a process for collecting statements from people involved in events or in the vicinity of events. An example of the type of initial information to gather is located in Appendix A at the back of this handbook.)

a. Record observations and findings as information is collected and reviewed.

b. Use basic means of recording information:

written notes

audiotape (this is not recommended, as it tends to make interviewees defensive)

pictorial (camcorder is ideal for recording the scene of the event)

c. All information should be properly identified:

source

date and time

location

basic content and purpose

name of person making record

  d. Don't rely on memory. Take complete notes. This ensures accuracy and completeness, facilitates report preparation, and has historical value.

  • Notes should be organized and dated.

  • Notes should be reviewed at the end of each day, updated, and analyzed.

Report the Problem (Obtain Feedback as Appropriate)

Keep in mind that you may need to report the problem at different times and to different people during your PIC process. See Chapter 9 for more guidance on reports.

Handbook Example: *Misposition of Switch 8G 176*—Define Problem

On December 28, 1995, at 0700, a switchman inadvertently left closed (8G 176). The closed switch maintained the high voltage line energized, contrary to the switching order and work plan.

Where:	XYZ Power Plant (switch yard)
When:	December 28, 1995, 0700
What:	switch (8G 176) was left closed
Who:	switchman
How:	inadvertent (?)

2

Task Analysis

The task analysis is the first tool you will use. It will tell you where the pitfalls are within the task you are evaluating. This will help you to ask the right questions during the interview. Ideally, the interview should be done ASAP, so don't slow down. Get to the task analysis.

Hint: If you are a subject matter expert on this task, you already know the pitfalls of the task and how it is supposed to be done. You may, therefore, skip this step. However, as subject matter expert, you should have done the task in the recent past, with the same conditions, tools, and equipment. If you haven't, then do the step.

What Is Task Analysis?

Task analysis is a method of dividing or breaking down a task into its steps or subtasks by identifying the sequence of actions, instructions, conditions, tools, and materials associated with the performance of a particular task. It focuses on the task steps and how they are performed. Task analysis is one of the first analyses you will want to perform when beginning problem-solving. It is used during virtually every root cause analysis, because most problematic situations involve task performance.

Task analysis requires a review of work documents, logs, technical manuals, and other documents to determine what the task was about, how it was to be performed, and the desired effect on the equipment. It may also require interviewing.

Why Do Task Analysis?

Task analysis will help you find out what was supposed to happen. You may then compare what should have happened to what actually happened. It will provide a performance baseline enabling you to identify where human or equipment performance was not to standard or where equipment failure or inappropriate human action contributed to or caused a problem. It will help you prepare your questions for the interviews you will be doing. Most important, you will understand how the task was supposed to happen.

When to Do Task Analysis

Perform task analysis shortly after being notified that you are expected to identify and solve a problem. Prepare and get to it—the quicker the better.

How to Do Task Analysis

There are two kinds of task analysis:

- Paper-and-pencil
- Walk-through

Frequently, the problem solver will perform parts of both. A description of, and the steps to performing, each type of task analysis follows.

Paper-and-Pencil Task Analysis

Paper-and-pencil task analysis is a method of dividing or breaking down a task, on paper, into its steps or subtasks and identifying the sequence of actions, instructions, conditions, tools, and materials associated with the performance of a particular task.

Use a task analysis worksheet to itemize, in sequence, all the steps or subtasks and associated instructions or procedures, conditions, tools, and materials. Later, in the interview step of the process, you can compare the required task performance to the actual task performance that occurred during the event/problem of interest.

There are six key steps to performing a paper-and-pencil task analysis, including:

Step 1. Obtain preliminary information, such as what the person was doing when the error occurred, the time of day, etc.

Step 2. Determine the scope of the analysis. Which will be the task of interest?

Example: The worker may have been doing a diesel engine startup, but the task of interest is checking lube oil level that is accomplished as part of the diesel engine startup.

Step 3. Obtain available information about the task requirements by reviewing documents and interviewing. These interviews are not with the persons involved in the event, but with subject matter experts.

- Study relevant procedure(s).
- Review technical drawings.
- Review technical manuals.
- Gather machinery.
- Interview personnel who have performed the task to obtain a clear description of how the task is performed.

Step 4. Divide the task of interest into component actions or steps, and write the step name or action in order of occurrence on the Task Analysis Worksheet in the "Required Actions" column.

Step 5. For each required action, identify who performs the action step and the equipment component and tools used, if any. Write this information on the worksheet.

Step 6. Review the analysis information, and formulate any questions for which you need to collect additional data.

A full-blown task analysis as is done for training purposes can be very time-consuming. Paper-and-pencil task analysis used in investigating a performance problem will usually be a relatively straightforward specification of key task features for a system and tasks already in place. Look at a small portion of the big picture—that area where the equipment failure or human performance is inappropriate. For example, training task analysis may analyze the task of disassembling, repairing, and reassembling a large pump, while a PIC task analysis may be interested only in the installment of a pump bearing.

You want an understanding of what happened and how the activity was performed.

- Identify information, controls and displays, materials, and other requirements for task performance.
- Identify potential questions concerning deficiencies in procedures, control display design, training, etc., you will ask when interviewing the individuals involved and other knowledgeable personnel.
- Gain an understanding of how the task being analyzed should be performed.
- Identify potential problems with the performance of the task, such as inadequate procedures, inappropriate plant conditions, etc.

TABLE 2-1.

Handbook Example: Task Analysis Worksheet (Example 1)

TASK ANALYSIS - MISPOSITION OF SWITCH 8G 176
(FIRST TRY - TAKE AND EXECUTE SWITCHING ORDER)

STEPS	WHO	REQUIRED ACTIONS	COMPONENT	TOOLS	REMARKS/QUESTIONS
1	Dispatcher	Calls plant to perform switching order		Phone and form	Switching order was written correctly
2	Switchman	Writes switching order	Switching order book		Switching order was written correctly
3	Switchman	Reads back switching order		Phone	Switching order was written correctly
4	Switchman	Verify correctness of drawings		Drawings	Switching order was written correctly
5	Switchman	Enters switch yard			
6	Switchman	Executes switching order		Tags	How execute switching order
7	Switchman	Calls back switching order complete		Phone	

Note: This is not very revealing. The problem area was not broken down to small steps. The task, execute switching order, is now further developed.

TABLE 2-2.

Handbook Example: Task Analysis Worksheet (Example 2)

TASK ANALYSIS - MISPOSITION OF SWITCH 8G 176
(SECOND TRY - EXECUTE SWITCHING ORDER)

STEPS	WHO	REQUIRED ACTIONS	COMPONENT	TOOLS	REMARKS/QUESTIONS
1	Switchman	Stop in front of equipment you plan to operate	Listed component	Switching order	Danger tag was on correct switch
2	Switchman	Verify switching order to equipment to operate	Component label	Switching order	Correct component
3	Switchman	Opens 8G 176	8G 176		Ask details of how? Why found closed?
4	Switchman	Disengage motor	Lever	Bar	
5	Switchman	Hang danger tag		Tags	How execute order?
6	Switchman	Verify switch position	Switch		How verified?

Note: This analysis breaks down the problem area of the task. The questions developed will be more appropriate.

Walk-Through Task Analysis

Walk-through task analysis is a second kind of task analysis. You actually go through a simulation of task performance. It is always recommended over paper-and-pencil task analysis when feasible to perform.

It is a method of task analysis in which personnel who ordinarily do the task conduct a step-by-step enactment of the task being evaluated for an observer without actually performing the task.

Note: The first three steps are similar to the paper-and-pencil task analysis.

Step 1. Obtain preliminary information about what the person was doing when the inappropriate action or equipment failure occurred.

Step 2. Determine the scope of the analysis. Ask yourself, what will be the task of interest?

Step 3. Obtain more information about the task requirements by reviewing documents and interviewing.

- Study relevant procedures.

- View system drawings, block diagrams, and P & I drawings.

- Review the training department's task analysis data, if available.

- Interview personnel who have performed the task to obtain a clear description of how the task is performed.

Step 4. Produce a guide outlining how the task of interest will be carried out, indicating the steps in performing the task and the key controls and displays so that:

- You will know what to look for.

- You will be able to record actions more easily.

(A procedure with key items underlined is the easiest way of doing this. The best guide is a completed task analysis worksheet as done in paper-and-pencil task analysis.)

Step 5. Familiarize yourself with the guide, and decide exactly what information you are going to record and how you will record it.

- You may simply want to check off each step and controls and displays as they occur. Discrepancies and problems may be noted in the margin or in an adjacent space provided for comments.

Step 6. Select personnel who normally perform the task. If the task is performed by a crew, crew members should play the same role they fulfill when carrying out the task.

Step 7. Observe personnel walking through the task, and record their actions and use of displays and controls. Note any discrepancies or problem areas.

Step 8. Summarize and consolidate any problem areas noted. Identify probable contributors to the inappropriate action.

Notes:

- Make the walk-through as real as possible. You are trying to understand what happened and how it happened to determine the human performance or equipment failure problem and how it contributed to the event.

- You may do walk-through task analysis or parts of it in slow motion, stopping the action if there are questions or having the personnel describe what they are doing, what controls and displays they are using, etc.

- You may do walk-through task analysis in real time to identify time-related problems. If you do this, do not interrupt the task performer during the task. Instead, ask him or her to clarify the steps after the task is complete. If time is not an issue in the task, you may interrupt to ask the performer to explain the steps as you watch each step.

- An alternate way of doing task analysis is simply to observe the actual task as it is being done. The advance preparation noted above is still necessary.

- The training department likely has job performance measures for many tasks. Check with them first to save the time it would take to create a guide or checklist of your own.

3

Change Analysis

What Is Change Analysis?

Change analysis is the comparison of an activity that has been success-fully performed to the same activity when it has been unsuccessfully performed. The tool is like comparing two task analyses and evaluating the differences. It is the process by which you compare and analyze what you expected would happen to what actually happened, paying particular attention to changes over time.

Always Ask These Questions

- What was different about this time from all the other times the same task or activity was carried out without an inappropriate action or equipment failure?
- Why now, not before?
- Why here, not there?

Why Do Change Analysis?

The difference between what happened on other occasions and what happened when things went wrong can well lead you to the root cause. Sometimes a single change, at other times several changes, will point you to the root or at least contributing cause(s).

A simple example may help bring this point home:

After moving your car, you see oil on the driveway where the car was parked. The car has never leaked oil before. The day before, you had the oil changed and a new oil filter installed at a different garage.

Where would you begin troubleshooting this problem? Obvi-ously, there has been a change—oil on the driveway.

27

Look at the change. Begin thinking of what could have happened. What was different this time compared to when it was done without any problems?

When to Do Change Analysis

Use change analysis when:

- The causes of the inappropriate action or equipment failure are obscure.
- You don't know where to start.
- You have started some evaluation steps and are stumped. Therefore, you don't know what else to do.
- You suspect a change may have contributed to the inappropriate action or equipment failure.

How to Do Change Analysis

Step 1. Study the situation with the inappropriate action or equipment failure. Write down the steps or actions taken when that task was performed.

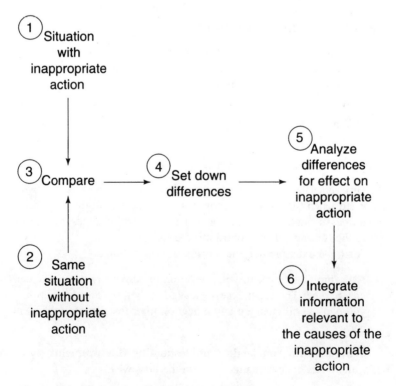

Figure 3-1. Six steps involved in change analysis.

Step 2. Consider a comparable situation that did not have an inappropriate action or equipment failure. Write down the steps or actions when that task was performed.

Step 3. Compare the two.

Step 4. Clearly write down all the differences. Use the change analysis worksheet.

Step 5. Analyze the list of differences for effects on the situation.

Step 6. Integrate all the data gained during the analysis. It may be useful to place the results of the change analysis on the Event and Causal Factor Chart that will be discussed later.

Use of Information Gained From Change Analysis

- Rarely can change analysis be used independently. Usually it is used in conjunction with other techniques and is integrated with event and causal factor charting.
- Change analysis can provide leads to follow up on.
- Change analysis can provide leads to use during interviews.

Pitfalls of Change Analysis

To use change analysis effectively, you need to be aware of the pitfalls it can involve. They are:

- Not recognizing gradual change.

  Example: The stroke time of a valve increases over time due to a corrosion buildup on the stem.

- Not identifying all the changes.

  Example: Personnel are not aware of how a design change affected the switching log.

- Not recognizing the domino or synergistic effects of changes made elsewhere.

  Example: Recently the lube oil heat exchangers for the main turbine were replaced so there would be more cooling water flow for the turbine lube oil coolers. Two buildings away and one floor up, the auxiliary operators began to experience difficulties with the instrument air compressors tripping whenever they were shifted. (Because the flow through the lube oil cooler was increased, there was insufficient water for both air compressors to be run together, as they would be when shifting, without receiving a low cooling water flow trip.)

- Incorrectly defining the change.

Figure 3-2. Handbook example: Misposition of switch 8G 176—Change analysis worksheet.

CHANGE FACTOR	DIFFERENCE/CHANGE	EFFECT	QUESTIONS TO ANSWER
WHAT (CONDITIONS, ACTIVITY, EQUIPMENT)	*Switch type (only motor operated G switch of type)*	*Different disengage operation*	*Disengage same?* *Switch labeled?* *Engaged labeled?*
WHEN (OCCURRENCE, PLANT STATUS, SCHEDULE)	*0700*	*Rush*	*Ask — if rushed.* *How long for task?* *How scheduling done?*
WHERE (PHYSICAL LOCATION, ENVIRONMENTAL CONDITIONS, STEP OF PROCEDURE)			*Weather?* *Glare of lights?* *Glare of sun?*
HOW (WORK PRACTICE, OMISSION, EXTRANEOUS ACTION, OUT OF SEQUENCE, POOR PROCEDURE)			*What was intent?* *How verified?*
WHO (PERSONNEL INVOLVED, SUPERVISION)	*Switchman and trainee*	*Experience LTA-?*	*Done task before?* *What did trainee do?*

4

Control Barrier
Analysis

Note: This is the first tool that identifies causes of an event. Some simple events need only a control barrier analysis for the whole evaluation.

What Is Control Barrier Analysis?

Control Barrier Analysis is a technique you use to analyze an activity or a process paying attention to where physical or administrative barriers are needed to prevent events or unwanted action. Your analysis locates where barriers were either missing or ineffective.

What Are Control Barriers?

What are some of the barriers designed and erected to reduce highway fatalities? You might well answer: seat belts, padded dashboards, divided highways. These would be physical control barriers. If you mention drivers' licenses, highway laws, road signs, or speed limits, you would be listing administrative control barriers.

Control barriers are administrative or physical aids that are made part of work conditions. They are devices employed to protect people and equipment and enhance the safety and performance of the man–machine system. They ensure consistent desired behavior; they enable personnel and equipment to perform consistently in keeping with requirements and expectations. When designing or investigating control barriers for human and equipment performance, you will find the causal factor categories in Chapter 7 very helpful.

Important tasks rarely rely on a single control barrier. Generally, control barriers are diverse and numerous—a defense-in-depth concept.

Control barrier analysis, then, is a method of finding and checking out the control barriers to see if they effectively performed their function of protecting people and enhancing the safety and performance of the human–machine interface.

The following examples of barriers highlight their importance:

Physical Control Barriers

Conservative design allowances

Engineered safety features

Fire barriers and seals

Ground fault protection devices

Locked doors, valves, breakers, and controls

Shielding/insulation

Redundant equipment

Safety and relief devices

Administrative Control Barriers

Safety Rules

Alarms and annunciators

Certification of engineers

Certification of technicians and workers

Maintenance work requests

Methods of communication

Operating and maintenance procedures

Policies and practices

Qualification of welders

Work permits

Regulations

Supervisory practices

Engineering specifications

Training and education

Licensing of workers

Why Do Control Barrier Analysis?

Control barrier analysis is done to determine if all the control barriers pertaining to the problem you are investigating are present and effective.

When to Do Control Barrier Analysis

There is no one right time. One strategy is to do a control barrier analysis as soon after task analysis as possible. Another strategy is to first become familiar with the task, its associated policies, procedures, and other documents; observe the actual scene; and interview subject matter experts. Then do control barrier analysis.

If control barriers perform their intended function, an event or inappropriate action should not occur. When barriers fail, they always fail in a series. If one control barrier performs its intended function, an event or inappropriate action should not occur. In reality, there is a weakness in every control barrier. If they line up, then a task failure will occur.

In investigating problems, think in terms of control barriers. Identify how control barriers failed, and provide recommendations on how to strengthen the existing control barrier or establish a new one.

Focus your efforts on the control barriers that control the primary effect and you will save valuable time. Use control barrier analysis in every situation you analyze.

Two Methods for Control Barrier Analysis

1. Stand-Alone Method
2. Integrated Method

The stand-alone method involves the identification and evaluation of all the applicable administrative and physical control barriers for the situation.

The integrated method involves superimposing control barriers into the Event and Causal Factor Chart (ECFC) as you develop it.

How to Do Control Barrier Analysis

Step 1. Identify all the existing administrative and physical control barriers pertaining to the problematic situation.

Note: If you are using the stand-alone method, you can use the Barrier Analysis Worksheet. If you are using the integrated method, you will show control barriers on the ECFC.

Step 2. Evaluate the effectiveness of each existing control barrier. Identify all apparent barriers that failed and allowed the event to progress. You will usually do this early in the investigation and continue your evaluation until completion.

Step 3. Determine how the barrier failed. For example, the procedural control barrier failed because although the procedure was correct, it was not used.

Step 4. Determine why the barrier failed. For example, the procedure was not used because the operator felt that the problem would be fixed soon; therefore, he did not feel it necessary to log in the deficiency.

Step 5. Identify where control barriers, had they existed, would have prevented the occurrence.

Step 6. With information learned from other sources, validate the results of control barrier analysis. The interviews will provide details as to how and why the barrier failed. A subject matter expert is a good source to validate your findings.

Pitfalls of Control Barrier Analysis

Consider at least three pitfalls:

1. If you do not recognize all of the failed control barriers that contributed to the event, the analysis may be incomplete. For this reason, it is recommended that you use control barrier analysis in conjunction with other root cause analysis tools, and integrate it on the event and causal factor chart.

2. If you have limited knowledge, background, and experience in the area of the problem, control barriers could be missed. For example, someone with experience in the maintenance area might miss nonapparent control barriers within the operations area.

3. This pitfall exists within the control barriers themselves. You might expect that most procedures at a work site would be pretty much standard. That might not be the case.

Regardless of variations in control barriers, PIC provides the framework for control barrier analysis because it focuses on precise control barrier categories (refer to Appendix B) that have proven to be keys to equipment and human performance problems.

Figure 4-1. Handbook example: Misposition of switch 8G 176—Control barrier analysis.

CONSEQUENCE(S)	BARRIER(S) THAT SHOULD HAVE PRECLUDED THE EVENT	BARRIER ASSESSMENT (WHY THE BARRIER(S) FAILED)
Switch closed	Switching order process	Did you think you opened the switch?
	Verification	How verified—trained? How labeled?
Switch motor engaged	Switchman's knowledge	Operated switch before?
	Switching order form	Did you follow form? Any problems?
	Labels	How labeled?
Trainee control LTA-?	Policy/training	What is policy/training?
(LIST ONE AT A TIME) NEED NOT BE IN SEQUENTIAL ORDER	(IDENTIFY ALL APPLICABLE PHYSICAL AND ADMINISTRATIVE BARRIERS FOR EACH CONSEQUENCE)	(IDENTIFY IF BARRIER WAS MISSING, WEAK, OR INEFFECTIVE AND WHY)

5

Event and Causal Factor Charting

What Is Event and Causal Factor Charting?

Event and causal factor charting is an analysis tool whereby you chart the relationship of events, conditions, changes, barriers, and causal factors on a timeline using standard symbols for each.

What Is an Event and Causal Factor Chart?

An event and causal factor chart (ECFC) is a flow chart that graphically displays an entire event. The heart of the ECFC is the sequence-of-events line. When developing the chart, you select the beginning and ending points to capture all essential information pertinent to the situation.

As you establish the event line, you add additional situational features, such as related conditions, secondary events, and presumptions.

Probable causal factors become evident as you develop the chart. Often causal factors that were not obvious at the outset become evident through this technique, making the ECFC a powerful root cause analysis tool.

The ECFC is particularly useful for complex and complicated situations and is more meaningful than long narrative descriptions.

The ECFC provides an excellent opportunity to graphically display control barriers, changes, and cause and effect, and to show how they were involved in equipment and human performance problems.

Why Construct an Event and Causal Factor Chart?

An event and causal factor chart has several benefits. It:

- organizes the situation and all the data involved with the analysis;
- shows the exact sequence of events from beginning to end and encourages the development of other conditions, secondary events, presumptions, causal factors, changes, primary events, and control barriers;
- uses results of barrier analysis and change analysis—these results may expand the sequence of events, but more important, they provide more meaningful information;
- presents the situation at a single glance (big picture);
- provides a cause-oriented explanation for the situation you are analyzing;
- helps ensure objectivity;
- helps organize quantitative information (e.g., time, temperature, height); and
- provides a basis for determining beneficial changes to prevent future similar problems.

Why Is Event and Causal Factor Charting So Effective?

Event and causal factor charting is effective because:

- equipment failure, conditions, and inappropriate human actions usually are associated with a set of successive events;
- inappropriate actions for human performance events occur during the conduct of some activities when barriers are defective or nonexistent;
- this type of charting captures the whole situation in one integrated format; and
- many (but not all) causal factors readily become evident.

When to Begin Constructing an ECFC

Begin as soon as you know what happened! Start a preliminary ECFC as you gather initial information, and add to it with each set of new information. You, as an evaluator, will be more prepared for each interview by continually updating the ECFC.

Definitions and Symbols

The following definitions are necessary to talk about interpreting and developing event and causal factor charts:

1. Event

An action or happening that occurs during some activity. Enclose all events (actions or happenings) in *rectangles.*

2. Primary event

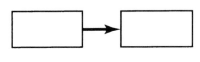

The action or happening directly leading up to or following the primary effect; shown as a *rectangle* on the primary event line. The primary sequence of events is depicted in a straight horizontal line with the primary events connected with a *heavy arrow.* Relative time sequence is generally left to right.

3. Undesirable event

An undesirable event (equipment failure/condition or inappropriate action) that was critical for the situation being analyzed to occur; shown as a *diamond.* e.g., component failures, system malfunctions.

4. Secondary event

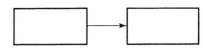

An action or happening that impacts the primary event but is not directly involved in the situation; shown as a *rectangle* below or above the primary event line. Connect secondary events by *small arrows.*

5. Terminal event

The end point of the analysis; shown as a *circle* at the end of the primary event line.

6. Conditions

Circumstances pertinent to the situation that may have influenced the course of events; shown as *ovals* connected to events. All conditions are connected to other conditions and/or events by *dotted arrows.*

7. Presumptive event

An action or happening that is assumed because it appears logical in the sequence but cannot be proven; shown as a *dotted rectangle.*

8. Causal factor

A factor that shaped the outcome of the situation; shown as a *solid oval with the right end shaded.*

9. Presumptive casual factor

A factor that is assumed because it appears to logically affect another condition or event; shown as a *dotted oval shaded at the right end.*

10. Secondary event sequences, contributing causal factors, and causal factors are depicted above or below the primary event line.

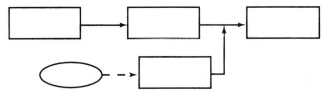

11. Barrier

Failed barrier

12. Change

Criteria for Event Description

You will use the following event (this is the little "e" event—see Glossary) description criteria when you develop an ECFC:

1. Events describe an action or happening, e.g., "pipe burst at 300 psig," and not "pipe weld had crack in it."

2. Events describe a *single* action or happening.

3. Each event in the sequence is described by a short sentence with *one* noun and *one* active verb.

4. Each event must be precisely described.

5. Events should be quantified when possible, e.g., "mechanic torqued bolt to 65 lbs." and not "mechanic torqued bolt."

6. Events are based on *valid* information (facts).

7. Chart scope ranges from beginning to end of the situation sequence.

8. Each event should logically follow from the one preceding it.

9. Consider the level of detail necessary when developing the event sequence.

Cause-and-Effect Analysis

Principles

1. All undesirable events are caused to happen. These events are the result of equipment failures, design problems, human performance errors, etc. These are shown as *primary effects* on the ECFC.

2. Because undesirable events are caused to happen, they are actually effects created by some additional cause(s). These are shown as contributing and root causes on the ECFC.

3. The root cause(s) of an event can be determined by using the cause-and-effect relationships that exist surrounding a primary effect (covered in detail in Chapter 7).

Using Cause and Effect

1. Use the ECFC to reconstruct a scenario, taking care to identify those undesirable events that should not have occurred (primary effects).

2. Examine these primary effects, and determine what conditions, or causes, allowed or forced each effect to occur. Place these conditions on the chart showing their relationship to the effect.

3. For each condition identified, ask why that condition existed, i.e., treat the condition as an effect and determine the cause(s). Incorporate these new conditions into the chart.

4. Repeat this cause-and-effect analysis until:

   • the cause is outside the control of the plant to correct;

   • the primary effect is fully explained;

- there are no other causes that can be found that explain the effect; and

- further cause-and-effect analysis will not provide additional benefit in correcting the initial problem.

Tips for Cause-and-Effect Analysis

1. Often, cause-and-effect analysis will lead to management-controlled root causes.

2. When more than one cause is responsible for an effect, each cause must be analyzed.

3. Cause-and-effect analysis is most effective when used within the framework of the ECFC. It is not a stand-alone method because the situation must first be unraveled to the point where all primary effects are identified. This is particularly true in situations involving multiple primary effects. Cause-and-effect analysis alone is not effective in identifying primary effects. The evaluator needs to consider all techniques, including cause-and-effect analysis, to determine primary effects and their causes.

4. Analyzing situations involving equipment failure and human performance is not an exact science. This process of cause-and-effect provides a logical, structured guide to maintaining the evaluation on track, but will require good judgment and experience to be effective.

How to Construct an ECFC

Step 1: Define scope of chart from initial information. (Some people find it easier to start with a simple timeline.)
   a. Initiating event (beginning point).
   b. Terminal event.

Step 2: Assess initial information and documentation.
   a. What was the primary effect(s) (the inappropriate action, component failure or system malfunction)?
   b. When did it occur (during what task/evaluation)?
   c. How did it occur?
   d. What were the consequences?

Step 3: Begin constructing the preliminary primary event line.
   a. Start early—use currently known facts.
   b Use self-stick removable notes.
   c. Set down the known sequence of primary events on the primary event line.

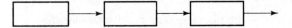

d. Insert secondary events and conditions into chart in the appropriate place.

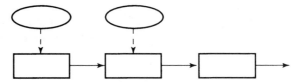

Step 4: Gather new facts and add to chart.
    a. Events—primary and secondary (depict above or below primary event line): as you proceed through the evaluation process, you will discover new information that should be inserted into the chart at the correct location to show its relation to the big picture. Use appropriate tools and techniques:

        interviewing

        root cause analysis techniques

        causal factor worksheets

    b. Identify conditions
        1) Initial (e.g., power level, time of day, number of workers).
        2) Leading to the primary effects (e.g., outdated procedure, problems with tools and communications equipment, frequent repair).
        3) After the primary effect occurred (e.g., response to a problem, compounding actions taken).

Step 5: Identify and add causal factors and failed barriers to chart.
    a. Integrate results from other analysis techniques:

        cause-and-effect analysis

        control barrier analysis

        change analysis

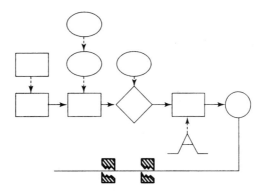

b. Decide which actions are inappropriate.

c. Verify that facts support conclusions.

Step 6: Identify corrective actions taken and needed.

a. Based upon failed barriers and causal factors.

b. Corrective actions must be supported by facts and be feasible.

TABLE 5-1.

Handbook Example: Misposition of Switch 8G 176—Event Timeline.

0655	dispatcher calls plant for switchman to perform switching order
0700	switchman writes switching order
0700	switchman reads back switching order
0703	switchman reviews drawings
0710	switchman enters switchyard
0715	switchman executes switching order
0720	switchman calls back switching order complete
0800	line crew arrives at work site
0803	fuzzes line, finds energized
0804	calls dispatcher
0810	switchman checks, finds switch shut—danger tag hung to keep switch open
0820	switchman/dispatcher writes new switching order and opens switch
0830	crew starts work

Figure 5-1. Handbook Example: Misposition of Switch 8G 176—Event and causal factor chart (Example 1).

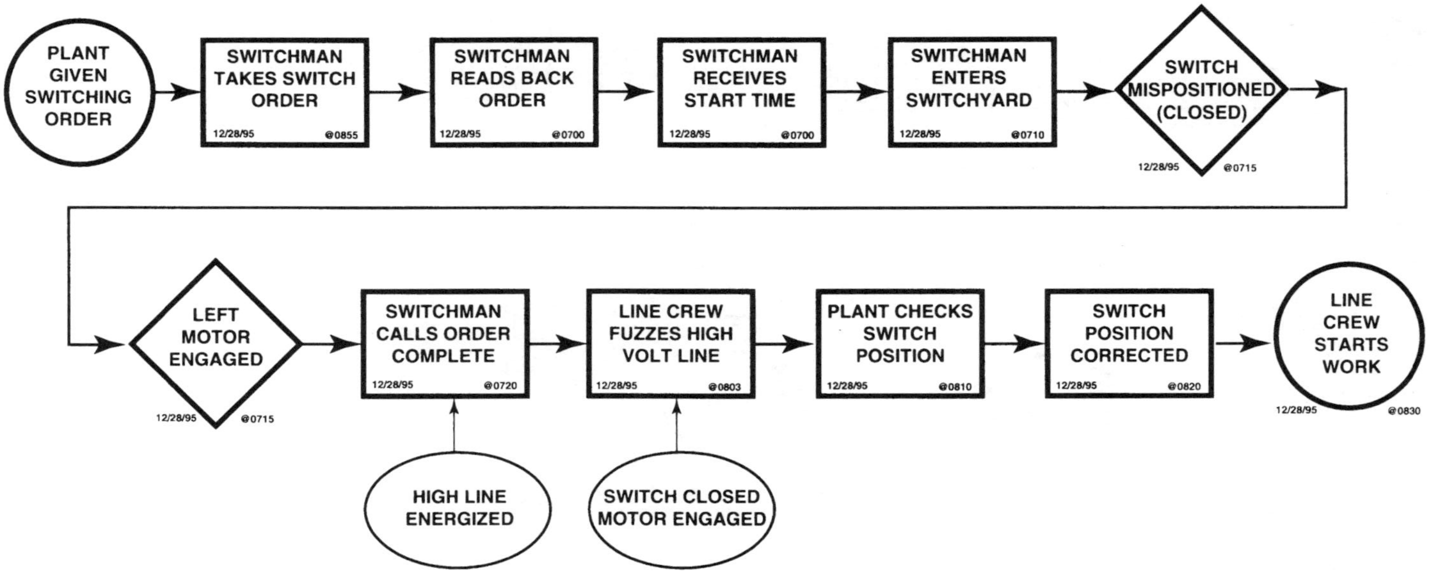

Figure 5-2. Handbook Example: Misposition of Switch 8G 176—Event and causal factor chart (Example 2, page 1).

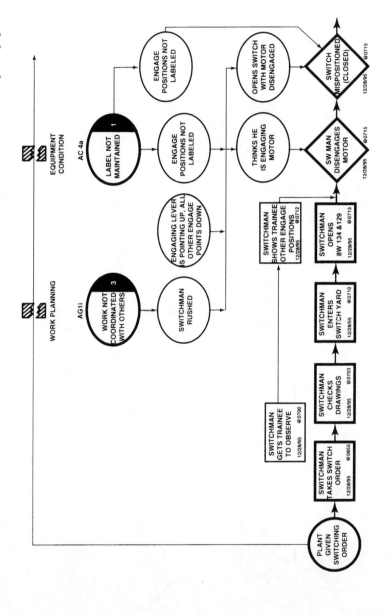

Figure 5-3. Handbook Example: Misposition of Switch 8G 176—Event and causal factor chart (Example 2, page 2).

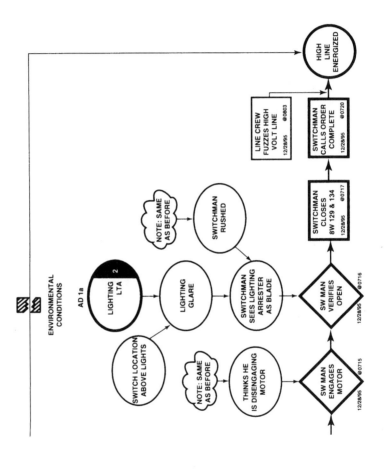

6

Interviews

Note: Interviews are performed through the remainder of the PIC process. Normally, your first interviews would be with persons who were not directly involved in the event, but are aware of the event because they are senior in the chain of command, or they observed the event without being involved. You should have a good idea of what happened and how it happened. When you interview the persons directly involved, your questions can be more focused and probing for causes of the event. This would correlate with Chapter 7 (Root Cause) in the process. As corrective actions are developed, the involved supervision will be consulted for feedback. Additionally, when you write your report, you would consult with the persons involved in the event and the appropriate supervision. These interviews have a totally different purpose.

Techniques for Conducting Interviews

Although the interview appears to be a continuous process from beginning to end, in reality it consists of four discrete stages:

Stage 1: Prepare for the interview.

Stage 2: Open the interview.

Stage 3: Conduct the interview.

Stage 4: Close the interview.

If you handle each stage thoughtfully and appropriately, you can maximize the opportunity to establish good rapport with the interviewee and to collect high-quality information.

Remember that your goal during interviewing is to find facts, not faults. Be objective and collect data without placing blame.

In the pages that follow, you will find suggestions on how to complete the four stages of the interview and on how to handle major issues during each stage.

Stage 1: Prepare for the Interview

Thorough preparation for an interview will help you successfully conduct the interview. When preparing, follow the steps described.

Step 1: Plan the Interview

Before beginning the interview:

1. Review any data previously collected, pertinent documents, and relevant system descriptions.
2. Write questions down to help keep the interview on track. If this is done beforehand, there is a better chance to word questions sensitively. Causal factor worksheets may help you formulate questions, as will task analysis and change analysis. If a control barrier analysis was performed, the questions may verify probable causes.
3. Determine how you will record your notes.
4. Schedule interviews allowing time between interviews to reconstruct notes and update the developing ECFC.
5. Plan on talking only 15% to 20% of the time. Listen 80% to 85% of the time.
6. Dress appropriately for the location.

Step 2: Plan to Answer Interviewee Questions

During the interview, the interviewee may request information. Be ready to answer these questions:

- Why do you want to talk with me?
- What will you do with what I tell you?
- Will my name be used?
- How long will this interview take?
- What is problem identification and correction?

Step 3: Establish the Physical Setting

Several settings may be available, including the following:

- Interviewee's boss's office
- Interviewee's work area with others around
- Interviewee's work area with no one else around
- Neutral areas—the best location

When establishing the physical setting, consider privacy and the possibility of interruptions. Interruptions interfere with concentration and disrupt rapport. Ensuring privacy and avoiding interruptions demonstrate the respect and concern of the company for the employee's rights and feelings. You should conduct the interview, if possible, in a closed room, where the employee can talk freely without worry about being overheard. Plan in advance to avoid interruptions—for example, post an interviewing sign and transfer all phone calls.

Stage 2: Open the Interview

The interview opening is very important because it sets the tone for the rest of the interview. The opening should accomplish the following:

- Put the interviewee at ease.
- Establish interviewer credibility.
- Show interest in the interviewee and the interviewee's job. Listening is the best way to show interest.
- Get the interviewee involved quickly.

When opening an interview, you should use the following steps.

Step 1: Greet the Interviewee

Initial courtesy will help ensure a quality flow of information later. Try to make the employee feel as comfortable as possible to reduce any tension that is present. Be pleasant and courteous regardless of your own mood at the time. Use the following techniques:

- Establish eye contact.
- Smile. A smile will communicate at least as much as what you say. People are often unwilling to talk openly to someone who is stone-faced and unresponsive. You should, of course, not overdo the smile or smile in a contrived, artificial manner.
- Use vocal expression. People often fail to use their voices effectively. Men, in particular, tend to speak in the lower register that can result in a strained monotone. It is important to use the entire vocal register to sound more interested, animated, and responsive. Monitor your pace to avoid talking too rapidly or too slowly.

Step 2: Exchange Small Talk

After greeting and seating the employee, a short period of informal conversation is a good way of getting things rolling. You could begin with a sincere compliment, a question to learn something about the interviewee, or an exchange of common past work experiences. This may be very short if the employee is already relaxed, confident, and ready to begin. If the employee is shy, inhibited, and withdrawn, an informal conversation may help to break the ice.

Step 3: State the Purpose of the Interview

Make a general opening statement summarizing the purpose of the interview and the problem identification and correction program. Include the approximate length of time the interview should take, and be prepared to stick to it.

Step 4: Answer Interviewee Questions

Give the interviewee an opportunity to ask any questions and thereby identify any concerns, issues, or fears he or she may have. Respond to all interviewee questions in some way. If you're unable to answer a question, say so instead of making up an answer.

Stage 3: Conduct the Interview

Interviewing can be mentally demanding on the interviewer. You are juggling many skills at the same time. You are trying to ask the right questions, listen to the responses, take notes, respond to human issues, and monitor the progress of the interview.

Many of your questions will probably net a great deal of information given in a more or less logical fashion. As you probe for more information, it is important that you try to form a mental picture about what happened and possibly what caused it to happen. This picture of what happened and what may have caused it to happen will help you probe in specific areas. The questions you then ask will help you to check out your ideas about possible causes. This is difficult to do; you must maintain your objectivity and be cautious that you do not follow just one possible cause and thereby miss important data.

Types of Interview Questions

First let's look at the difference between closed and open-ended questions and then take a closer look at five different types of questions.

Closed questions require only a "yes" or "no" from the interviewee. Avoid them, as they set the tone for further short responses, require you to say too much yourself, and encourage you to formulate conclusions with which the interviewee can concur. For example, don't say:

"That accident was caused by . . . , wasn't it," or

"Do you know what caused that accident?"

Open-ended questions encourage the interviewee to respond with more than a "yes" or "no" and begin with an open-ended word (e.g., what, when, relate, describe). These questions elicit a great deal of information from the interviewee. For example:

"What caused the accident?"

"How did it come about?"

"Tell me some more about that . . ."

"Give me some details regarding . . ."

"Describe the situation that led to . . ."

The purpose of writing down the questions is to ensure that they are sensitively worded. This will help keep the interviewee from becoming defensive. Writing down the questions also keeps the interview on track and prevents overlooking areas you wanted to cover. Asking different types of questions sounds more natural than repeating the same type of question. To be an effective interviewer, there are several different types of questions you can use and one to avoid.

- **Use** exploratory questions.
- **Use** follow-up questions.
- **Use** comment questions.
- **Avoid** leading questions.

Exploratory Questions

Exploratory questions use phrases such as "suppose you tell me" and encourage the interviewee to provide both comprehensive and in-depth information. Use exploratory questions to open a questioning sequence. Examples are:

"What can you tell me about . . . ?"

"What can you recall from . . . ?"

Follow-Up Questions

Open-ended questions may produce information that is weak in some areas. In fact, the response may be completely unclear. For example, when the answer deals with an unfamiliar work area or equipment, you will need to follow up or clarify the comments. You could ask:

"What do you mean by . . . ?"

"Tell me more about . . ."

"What is . . . ?" and so forth.

If the comment is completely understandable but inadequate in content, follow-up questions help complete the picture. It may be necessary to ask:

"How did this come about?"

"How did other workers respond?"

"Who else knew about this?"

When using follow-up questions, ask whatever is necessary to complete your picture of the incident.

Comment Questions

A variation on the follow-up question is the comment question. Comments are often better at eliciting information than questions because they seem more natural and less blatant. Examples include:

"Tell me more about that."

"Give me some more detail regarding . . ."

These comments encourage elaboration of points that have been made earlier without seeming like a question. They also show the interviewer's interest.

Leading Questions

Avoid leading questions! They put words into the interviewee's mouth or unintentionally tell him or her how to respond. Examples include:

"This was only a minor problem, wasn't it?"

"You tried to do something, didn't you?"

"I suppose you went through the proper channels with your complaint."

Rather than encouraging the interviewee to give information openly, leading questions make it difficult to answer honestly.

Techniques for Asking Questions and Responding to Answers

Probing Technique

You can use a two-step probing technique to get the depth of information required.

- The first question is exploratory, general, and open-ended, eliciting descriptive details.
- The second follow-up question begins with "why" or asks for an evaluation or opinion of what happened.
- Alternate ways to begin the second question are: "How do you explain . . ." or "What do you think caused that . . . ?"

For example:

"Tell me something about the maintenance problems in the Fuel Handling Building" followed by "Why do you think the welds were improperly done?"

The two-step probing technique can yield vital information, but you should use it sparingly or the interviewee will feel drilled. Reserve it for the important areas.

Two-step probing has been compared to prospecting for uranium—you cover a broad area with the Geiger counter, then dig into the earth only when something important has been detected during the general search.

Other Techniques for Asking Questions and Responding to Answers

1. Begin with open-ended questions so that the interviewee can describe things in his or her own way. This will elicit the greatest amount of information up front.

2. Begin questioning in the same tone of voice as you used in the greeting. Avoid suddenly becoming serious and intent. Try to make a smooth transition from the greeting to the introductory questions stage.

3. Assume a permissive general manner to encourage complete answers. This includes nodding the head, saying "I see," "uh-huh," "okay," etc., and giving the impression of responsiveness and attentiveness.

4. Never show surprise at anything the interviewee says, never disagree, and never appear to cross-examine; otherwise, the employee is likely to begin screening and editing responses.

5. Try to show understanding, even if you disagree. Compliment answers or make comments where appropriate.

6. Avoid interrupting, at least initially; you can focus the interview later.

7. Make it possible for the employee to discuss unfavorable personal actions (if they have occurred) by showing understanding. It is possible to allow the employee to save face without

appearing to condone negative behaviors. Confront sensitive issues honestly.

8. Permit a slight pause in the conversation at times. This is a powerful technique for drawing out the employee. Avoid pausing too frequently or too long (allow no more than 8 to 10 seconds of silence.)

9. When appropriate, let the mood lighten a bit so that it doesn't become deadly serious. However, avoid telling jokes or anecdotes. They interrupt the employee.

10. Talk the interviewee's language. Note the vocabulary, degree of formality, education level, etc., that the interviewee uses and speak at this level yourself. Speaking beyond the employee's level of comprehension, or at an offensively low level, will inhibit trust and information-gathering.

11. Ask questions with a purpose. Keep mentally ahead of the employee, and be ready to ask appropriate questions as they are needed. Avoid meaningless questions.

12. Follow a systematic approach to gathering data. Determine exactly what happened, when, how, who was responsible, etc.

13. Summarize throughout the interview. This may elicit more information, provide clarification, and ensure you understand all the interviewee's concerns.

14. Monitor the interviewee's nonverbal cues to assess how the interview is going and adjust if necessary. For example, ask brief questions, clarify less, listen more.

Note: Use the above techniques naturally and comfortably, or they will be apparent and interfere with the interview.

The Communication Process

At the heart of interviewing is the communication process. Understanding the communication process will help you improve your interviewing skills.

Communication is the process of sending and receiving messages. The diagram below shows a sender who "encodes" a message using words, voice inflection, and body language and a receiver who "decodes" or interprets the same message. Because communication is a two-way process, the receiver "encodes" a return message, sometimes called feedback, that the new receiver (the first sender) must "decode." While receivers may use all their senses to receive messages, they use hearing and sight the most. You can see that listening is an important component of the communication process.

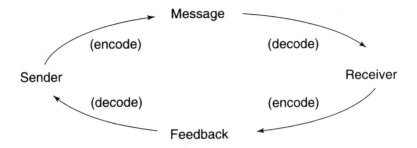

Research has shown that only one in four messages in interpersonal and organizational communication gets through as intended. There are many possible reasons for this.

Reasons for Miscommunication

- Receivers have their own messages and counter-messages that fight for predominance.
- The words chosen to communicate the message may not have meaning for the receiver.
- The environment distracts from listening and watching.
- The sender's emotions and body language may override or undermine the sender's words.
- Receivers have poor listening skills.

Improving listening takes effort and practice. Understanding some common listening problems and practicing their solutions may help.

Listening Problems

Many people experience listening problems when interviewing. Following are six common listening problems and suggested solutions.

PROBLEM	SOLUTIONS
1. Visual distractions	a. Maintain eye contact.
	b. Concentrate on the message.
2. Audible distractions	a. Reduce noise level.
	b. Select interview location carefully.
3. Interviewer is too talkative	a. Ask a question, then wait for the answer.
	b. Ask only important questions.

4. Interviewer jumps to conclusions	a. Listen to the answer before judging.
	b. Concentrate on recording facts; save interpretation for later.
5. Interviewer prejudges	a. Don't allow prejudice to influence your thinking.
6. Interviewer is closed-minded	a. Evaluate every response for logic, clarity, and accuracy.

Body Language

Both the sender and receiver use nonverbal messages, or body language. The sender enhances the message with body language; the receiver "reads" body language to add to the meaning of the words. During interviewing, body language is important for the feedback it provides to the interviewer. Nonverbal messages express degree of interest in the discussion, comfort with the topic, and level of assertiveness. Nonverbal messages provide a general indication of the degree of like or dislike and agreement or disagreement.

Some examples include the following:

Voice	Body
Pitch	Facial expression
Rate	Gestures
Volume	Posture

You can often interpret messages through nonverbal signals. For example:

- Looking down—hopeless
- Looking away—out of here
- Crossed arms or ankles—"circle the wagons"
- Rubbing chin—thinking about it
- Foot kicking—anger
- Hands on hips—meet the judge
- Feet on desk—meet the boss
- Leaning forward—anxious, keen interest, or exerting pressure
- Leaning backward—keeping a distance
- Slouching in chair—not interested

By reading nonverbal messages, you can determine how the interview is going. If you determine it is not going as well as you would like, you can make adjustments.

Remember that body language signals are not absolute messages. You must take them in context with the overall interview. A clear signal, however, is an abrupt change in body language. This could signal that you touched a sensitive topic.

Pitfalls of Interviewing

There are several pitfalls in interviewing, but the three most common are:

1. An overtalkative interviewer
2. An interviewee who becomes defensive
3. An over-talkative interviewee

Here are some suggestions for handling the pitfalls:

The Overtalkative Interviewer

- Plan good exploratory questions, and stick to the questions you planned to ask.
- Carefully consider the need for follow-up and probing questions.
- Concentrate on listening to the answers and taking notes.
- Don't repeat everything the interviewee says; summarize and clarify as needed.

Do you recognize yourself as an overtalkative person generally? Are there additional techniques you use that are effective?

The Defensive Interviewee

If, during an interview, the interviewee becomes defensive, it is probably because he or she perceives a threat or distrusts the interviewer. In either case, the interviewer needs to determine promptly the probable cause of the defensive behaviors and the appropriate approach to ease the interviewee's defensiveness. For example, the interviewer may:

- transmit supportive messages to enhance cooperation;
- reiterate the purpose of the interview and the importance of the interviewee's data to the overall correction of the problem; and/or
- address the defensive behaviors and ask questions about the nature of the threat.

When addressing the defensive behaviors, do so gently. If the interviewee does not trust you, addressing his or her behaviors may only heighten the mistrust.

If these methods do not work, the interviewer should decide to terminate the interview. The interviewer can reschedule a follow-up interview later, if necessary. The passing of time may ease the defensiveness.

The Overtalkative Interviewee

- Ask the interviewee to provide brief answers.
- Ask the interviewee to summarize what he or she has just said.
- Recall the time limit set for the interview, and indicate you have several other questions to ask.
- Use closed questions only as a last resort.

What are some other effective ways to handle an overtalkative interviewee?

Stage 4: Close the Interview

Just as you took care in preparing for, opening, and conducting the interview, you need to use the same care in closing the interview. To be successful in the close, complete each of these steps:

Step 1: Ease It to a Halt

Ask any final questions and check to make sure that all of the necessary information has been obtained. Ask the employee if he or she has any further comments or questions.

Step 2: Summarize the Complete Interview

This will make sure your impressions and information accurately reflect the interviewee's opinion. Share your notes with the interviewee.

Step 3: Thank the Interviewee

If the interviewee seems to want to prolong the meeting, there may be information of a sensitive nature he or she wishes to discuss. Probe gently regarding possible as yet undisclosed issues. Then express your appreciation for their time and honesty.

Following is a sample summary of collected data and completed data collection sheets. They include data about the event used in all the samples throughout this handbook.

PIC INTERVIEW SHEET

Interview Location: *Conference Room/Switchyard*

INTERVIEWEE	**INTERVIEWER**
Name: *John Dunn*	Initials: *MAA*
Job Title: *701 Switchman*	Date/Time: *12/29/95 0500*
Dept./Loc.: *Operations*	Card/Page: *1* of *2*

QUESTIONS:

1) Tell me about the switching order of 8G 176.

   Called late on mid shift— had to get done to support work for morning - took trainee to see how it was done—I performed the switching order—I finished and went home.

2) How was the switching order executed?

   I did it step by step. just like the form called for.

3) How was the switch position verified?

   I looked up and saw the blade pointing straight up in the air.

4) Tell me how the switch and motor positions were labeled?

   I don't recall.

5) What do you think caused the switch to be closed and the motor engaged?

   I have no idea. I'm sure I did it correctly.

6) What recommendations would you suggest?

   I don't know.

7) ...

Figure 6-1. Handbook example: Misposition of switch 8G 176—PIC interview sheet.

```
┌─────────────────────────────────────────────────────────────┐
│                   PIC OBSERVATION SHEET                       │
│ Location:  Switchyard                                         │
├───────────────────────────────┬───────────────────────────────┤
│   OBSERVEE (if applicable)     │           OBSERVER            │
│ Name: John Dunn                │ Initials: MAA                 │
│ Job Title: 701 Switchman       │ Date/Time: 12/29/95  0600     │
│ Dept./Loc.: Operations         │ Card/Page: 2 of    2          │
└───────────────────────────────┴───────────────────────────────┘
```

OBSERVATIONS:

entered switch yard with John Dunn to perform a walk through of the task

noticed there are no labels to identify switch position on motor engagement

can't see motor engagement—it's enclosed in sleeve

John points out that the motor is disengaged, just like he had found it yesterday. He had to engage the motor before he opened the switch.

after opening switch he raised (disengaged) the motor lever

John points out that the "dog ear" he locked open is in the same position as when he had it yesterday. But right now it is shut and in that position. He thinks something is broken or something. He thinks that may be why the switch didn't open.

"how did you verify switch position?" looked up through the lights to view blade. "look there, see it looks open now, see, told you I saw it pointing straight up."—What he saw and was pointing to was a lighting arrester.—he starts doubting what he saw. confusion . . .

Figure 6-2. Handbook example: Misposition of switch 8G 176—PIC observation sheet.

7

Determine Root Cause

Root cause determination is the process you use to systematically detect and analyze the possible causes of a problem in order to determine corrective action(s). During root cause analysis, you rely heavily on internal logic and reasoning skills (thinking) to reach conclusions. By making thinking visible through tools like lists, worksheets, and charts, you have information to show assumptions and test conclusions.

Data + Analysis = Information

You would not deliberately recommend corrective actions that result in unnecessary or cumbersome procedures, processes, or restrictions. You could, however, come to poor conclusions as a result of faulty reasoning or inaccurate and incomplete data.

What Is the Purpose of "Determine the Root Cause(s)"?

The purpose of this step in the PIC process is to collect and analyze data to determine *why* the problem occurred—the root cause(s)—so that the appropriate corrective action can be planned and implemented. You determine root causes by analyzing the data you have collected.

Root cause analysis has several goals:

- to determine presumptive causes of the performance problem (equipment, procedures, personnel, and work processes);
- to eliminate apparent and presumptive causes that data do not support;
- to select causes that need verification; and
- to determine root and contributing causes that need corrective action.

Achieving the goals will provide focus for corrective actions.

What Are the Types of Causes?

During PIC, you refer to causes of a problem in several different ways, including:

Presumptive cause(s)—cause(s) that may be apparent at the beginning of the investigation or that emerges during the data collection process. These are hypotheses that would explain the effects of the problem, but that *need validation.*

Contributing cause(s)—cause(s) that alone would not have caused the problem but is important enough to be recognized as needing corrective action to improve the quality of the process or product. (Includes secondary and possible causes.)

Root cause—the most basic reason for a problem, which, if corrected, will prevent recurrence of that problem.

Why Is It Important to Determine the Root Cause?

It is important to distinguish between the primary or root cause and the contributing causes in order to develop the necessary corrective actions to prevent the problem from reoccurring. Without thorough investigation of the problematic situation, you may initiate corrective action that does not eliminate or alleviate the problem and wastes valuable resources.

When to Determine the Root Cause

Once you have defined the problem based on facts, you can focus your root cause analysis efforts, plan a strategy, and begin to obtain the data needed to hypothesize and test possible causes.

How to Determine the Root Cause(s)

Plan a Root Cause Analysis Strategy

Once you have defined the problem, you will need to plan a strategy for determining the root cause. You may organize or reorganize your data, reassess your PIC strategy, and determine what action would be appropriate to collect additional needed data. You may need to decide on additional people to involve. In light of your problem definition, there may be additional reporting requirements.

If you have performed all the previous steps in the PIC process, you should be in good shape. But, if you skipped any, and now you know what happened, how it happened, but can't figure out why it happened, go back to the skipped steps. Pay particular attention to change analysis. Change analysis looks at the event in a way that exposes possible causes. See Chapter 3.

Collect and Analyze Data About the "Why?"

Root cause analysis is an iterative process. The successful problem solver must be able to assess the impact of each new piece of evidence and to integrate the new information into the analysis documents. To be able to return to any point in the investigation, the investigator must systematically document:

- the sequence of all relevant events;
- the source of all facts used as evidence;
- the basis of all assumptions;
- the reasons for all conclusions; and
- the sources (personal documents) of data.

Root Cause Analysis Tools

Problems and events can be very complex. Frequently, one event may involve multiple human errors, equipment failures, and/or procedural deficiencies. To properly evaluate such occurrences, special tools and techniques have been developed to systematically diagnose an event and determine its cause. The most commonly used root cause analysis tools are:

- Event and causal factor charting
- Control barrier analysis
- Fault tree analysis (may use causal factor worksheets or other)

Used singularly or in combination, these tools and the causal factor list help the problem solver show and document relationships, draw conclusions, and complete a thorough and systematic analysis of causes. Below is more information on the causal factor lists (you'll find copies in Appendix D).

Causal Factor Lists

Using these lists represents a method of logically stratifying possible event causal factors for human and equipment performance problems. The primary uses for the causal factor lists are:

- as a planning guide at the beginning of the investigation;
- as a source of intermediate analysis to determine the need for additional information; and

- as a means to determine root cause(s) once the preliminary ECFC has been constructed.

To create the causal factor list, simply identify the applicable causal factors from the detailed list in Appendix B. Either write down or make a computer file of the relevant factors. You may want to create a computer file or database containing all the factors in the appendix, which you can search as necessary.

Of the 19 causal factor categories, the first 12 relate to human performance, the next 6 relate to equipment performance, and the last category is for all external causes. The list that follows provides the category title and a description of the category. Appendix B details the list further.

Causal Factor Category List

Causal Factor Categories: Human

1. Verbal communication: the spoken presentation or exchange of information

2. Written procedures and documents: the written presentation or exchange of information

3. Man–machine interface: the design of equipment used to communicate information from the plant to a person (displays, labels, etc.)

4. Environmental conditions: physical conditions of work area

5. Work schedule: factors that contribute to the ability of the worker to perform his assigned task in an effective manner

6. Work practices: methods workers use to ensure safe and timely completion of task

7. Work organization/planning: the work-related tasks including planning, scoping, assignment, and schedule of the task to be performed

8. Supervisory methods: techniques used to directly control work-related tasks; in particular, a method used to direct workers in the accomplishment of tasks

9. Training/qualification: how the training program was developed and the process of presenting information on how a task is to be performed prior to accomplishing the task

10. Change management: the process whereby the hardware or software associated with a particular operation, technique, or system is modified

11. Resource management: the process whereby manpower and material are allocated for a particular task/objective

12. Managerial methods: an administrative technique used to control or direct work-related plant activities, which includes the process whereby manpower and material are allocated for a particular objective

Causal Factor Categories: Equipment

13. Design configuration and analysis: the design layout of system or subsystem needed to support plant operation and maintenance

14. Equipment condition: the failure mechanism of the equipment is the physical cause of the failure

15. Environmental conditions: the physical conditions of the equipment area

16. Equipment specification, manufacture, and construction: the process that includes the manufacture and installation of equipment in the plant

17. Maintenance/testing: the process of maintaining components/systems in optimum conditions

18. Plant/system operation: the actual performance of the equipment or component when performing its intended function

Causal Factor Category: External

19. External: human or nonhuman influence outside the usual control of the company

Determine Causes of Event

Draw Conclusions About the Root Cause(s)

With your data organized using one or more analysis tools, you should be able to draw conclusions about the root cause and produce the expected product—a clear description of the causes of the event including the primary or root cause and contributing causes. The process you use to determine the root and contributing causes typically includes the following steps:

1. Hypothesize or formulate presumptive causes.
2. Test/validate presumptive causes (an internal reasoning process).
3. Separate root causes from contributing (secondary or possible) causes.
4. Verify root causes (an external checking process).

Let's look at each of these steps in a little more detail.

Hypothesize or Formulate Presumptive Causes

As you investigate, you have been trying to determine the cause of the situation. In order to separate all the causes, it is helpful to phrase cause statements that clearly show both the cause and the effect(s) of the problem or problems inherent in the situation or event.

In our case of the misposition of switch 8G 176, cause statements might be:

- Insufficient time was allotted for the task, causing the switch-man to overlook key elements of the task.

- The difference in configuration of this switch compared to all other motor-operated switches in the yard opens the possibility for any switchman to misjudge the engagement of the switch motor.

- The absence of labels on the switch positions and motor engagement positions requires operators to make assumptions about the identification of each, causing possible improper identification.

Test/Validate Presumptive Causes

This step centers around the use of information and reasoning to support or eliminate presumptive causes. This is the heart of the analysis. The process is internal. You use reasoning skills based on logic. Two phrases may help you reason through the information:

1. For each cause, ask, "If I fix this, will I prevent the problem from happening again?"
2. For each cause, ask, "If (blank) is the root cause, how does it explain the problem situation as well as the comparable situations?"

If fixing that cause will not prevent the problem from recurring, or if that cause does not explain both the problem and comparable situations, then you can't consider it to be a root cause of the problem. You can now show it as a contributing cause on the ECFC.

Separate Root Causes From Contributing Causes

You will use three criteria to determine if each validated cause is a root cause or a secondary or possible cause:

1. The problem would not have occurred had the cause not been present.

2. The problem will not recur due to the same causal factor if the cause is corrected or eliminated.

3. Correction or elimination of the cause will prevent recurrence of similar conditions.

You can "operationalize" these criteria by converting them to questions. If you get a "yes" to a question, you have a root cause. If you get a "no," you have a contributing cause. For example, in our sample event, if a cause is no labels on the motor disconnect, ask, "Would the problem not have occurred had the motor disconnect been labeled?"

Verify Root Causes

This step will not be necessary with every problem. However, when doubts remain or you still have questions after you have tested the causes, you can use this external check on your analysis. In all cases, use a subject matter expert to verify your causes. This is a good sanity check. Other methods used to verify root causes are:

- Cross-check all facts for consistency
    witnesses
    physical evidence
    records and software
    expert testimony
    general physical: engineering information
    general historical: analytic information
- Cross-check all analyses using verified facts
    barrier analysis
    change analysis
    event and causal factor analysis
    others
- Resolve inconsistencies and discrepancies

Also, you can implement corrective action(s) on a trial basis to check your conclusions.

Report the Root Cause(s), as Appropriate

Keep in mind that you may need to report the cause(s) of the problem event at different times and to different people during the PIC process. Keep the appropriate management aware of your progress and findings. If done well, your report will generate no surprises or arguments at the end.

Handbook Example: *Misposition of Switch 8G 176*—Determine Root Cause

The primary cause of the event related to *man–machine interface;* specifically, the switch and the motor engaged positions were not labeled. The labeling program is weak. Many labels appear to be missing.

Contributing and possible causes include the following: *work organization/planning*—insufficient time was allotted for the task. The switchman started the task at 0700 and was relieved from the shift at 0730; *environmental conditions*—the switchman had to view the open switch by viewing it through the overhead lights. He could only see a silhouette.

8

Develop Corrective
Actions

What Is the Purpose of "Develop Corrective Action(s)"?

The purpose of this step in the PIC process is to identify all the corrective actions required to prevent the problem from recurring, or greatly reduce the probability that the problem will recur. This effort involves identifying and evaluating alternative corrective actions for each root cause and selected contributing causes, and selecting the corrective actions you will recommend.

What Are Corrective Actions?

Corrective actions are the countermeasures you take against the root or contributing causes. The goal of corrective action is to alleviate or reduce the probability that the problem will recur due to the same root cause.

During PIC, you may refer to action taken in response to solving a problem in two other ways besides "corrective action(s)":

Adaptive action is that immediate action you take to deal with the problem before thoroughly investigating the root cause(s). The goal of adaptive action is to allow you to live with the effects of the event or minimize additional damage as a result of the problem occurring.

Monitoring action is that action you take to check the effectiveness of your corrective action(s). The goal is to inform you if the corrective action is not working or if the problem is recurring due to some new root cause that was not identified earlier.

Why Is It Important to Develop Corrective Action(s)?

It is important to carefully develop and implement corrective action(s) for each root cause and selected contributing causes so your corrective actions have the broadest generic implications, ensure safety, are economically sound, and have a high reliability to prevent recurrence.

When to Develop Corrective Action(s)

Once you have identified and verified the root and contributing causes of a problem, you can begin to identify alternative corrective action(s).

How to Develop Corrective Actions

When you defined the problem and determined the root cause(s), some corrective actions became obvious. For example, in the misposition of switch 8G 176, obvious corrective actions involve scheduling practices and equipment.

Now is the time to organize and assess any existing information about each potential corrective action. You may need additional information in order to properly evaluate each alternative before you recommend.

Collect and analyze data to accomplish the following:

1. Formulate alternative corrective action(s) for each root cause.
2. Formulate alternative corrective action(s) for selected contributing causes.
3. Evaluate alternative corrective action(s).
4. Select recommended corrective action(s)

Formulate Corrective Action(s) for Root and Contributing Causes

Some corrective actions will be apparent. For example, if you found a procedure error to be the cause, you will recommend changing the procedure. For others less apparent, consider the causal factor categories you identified and your control barrier analysis.

Considerations for Evaluating Alternatives
Evaluate Alternatives and Select Corrective Actions

Ask the following *questions* about each corrective action to ensure it is viable. If it is not, formulate and evaluate a new corrective action.

- Will the corrective action(s) prevent recurrence of the condition?
- Is the corrective action within the capability of the company to implement?
- Does the corrective action allow us to meet our primary organizational objective (for the XYZ power plant, the safe and reliable production and distribution of power)?
- Have assumed risks been clearly stated?
- Is the corrective action compatible with other commitments?
- Will the corrective action have any adverse effects on the man–machine interface?

Also, consider the impact on other plant organizations, resources, and schedule. Consider the following issues to help you evaluate each alternative.

Impact on Other Plant Organizations

In formulating appropriate corrective actions, you must consider not only the impact the corrective action will have on the root cause(s), but the impact it will have on other plant organizations. For example, if a plant group that will implement the corrective action(s) already is understaffed and has more commitments that it can meet, your new recommendations, while required, may put undue hardship on the group. As part of the formulation of corrective action, you should consult the implementing groups. Rather than slow you down, this consideration will make the decision more effective. Ask yourself, "What impact will the development and implementation of the corrective actions have on other work groups?"

Some work groups to consider are:

Plant engineering	Design engineering
Quality control	Maintenance
Security	Health physics
Operations	Training
Drafting	Drawing control
Materials management	Document control
Licensing	Chemistry
Computer support	Modifications
Safety reviews	Configuration management

Impact on Resources

Try using the following questions:

- What is the cost (capital and O & M) of implementing the corrective actions?
- What resources are required for successful development of the corrective actions?
- What resources are required for successful implementation and continued effectiveness of the corrective actions?

Impact on Schedule

Here are additional questions you can use:

- In what time frame can the corrective actions reasonably be implemented?
- Will training be required as part of the implementation, and will training impact schedule?

Impact on Regulatory Commitments

Ask these questions:

- Will implementation of corrective action negate a commitment to the regulator?
- Will corrective action create a new regulatory commitment?

To Ensure the Adequacy of Your Selected Corrective Action(s)

Consider the following questions:

- Do the corrective actions address all the root causes?
- Will the corrective actions cause detrimental effects?
- What are the consequences of implementing the corrective actions?
- What are the consequences of *not* implementing the corrective actions?

Countermeasures Matrix

Use a Countermeasures Matrix

When evaluating your proposed corrective actions, you might find it helpful to assess both the effectiveness and feasibility of your actions (corrective, adaptive, and monitoring). You could choose to show your assessment in a matrix. For example, in the titanium hydrating case in Figure 8-1, each countermeasure was rated on a scale of 1 to 5, 1 being low and 5 being high. The ratings were then multiplied for an overall score. Such a system might help you prioritize your actions. Can you think of other ways to accomplish this?

Action Plan

Prepare and Distribute an Implementation Action Plan

Action plans should reflect all the information needed by accountable personnel to effectively implement the corrective actions. Include in your plan the necessary details for both implementation and monitoring.

WHAT - Scope of the work and specific activities

HOW - Activities in sequence and resources required

WHEN - Time frame, milestone dates

WHO - Responsible persons accountable for each activity

WHERE - Work locations, facilities

Assess Effectiveness

1. Determine how to monitor the effectiveness of corrective action(s).

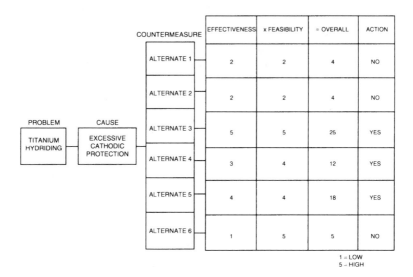

COUNTERMEASURE	EFFECTIVENESS	x FEASIBILITY	= OVERALL	ACTION
ALTERNATE 1	2	2	4	NO
ALTERNATE 2	2	2	4	NO
ALTERNATE 3	5	5	25	YES
ALTERNATE 4	3	4	12	YES
ALTERNATE 5	4	4	18	YES
ALTERNATE 6	1	5	5	NO

PROBLEM — TITANIUM HYDRIDING

CAUSE — EXCESSIVE CATHODIC PROTECTION

1 = LOW
5 = HIGH

Figure 8-1. Countermeasures matrix.

2. Confirm corrective action(s) are solving the problem.

3. Communicate results, as appropriate.

4. Take additional action, as appropriate.

Determine How to Monitor the Effectiveness of Corrective Action(s)

Typically, this would be done by monitoring for repeat problems. Monitoring may also include establishing and using indicators to regulate processes, tasks, or activities of personnel or equipment, checking performance results using these indicators, and taking appropriate action. You need to determine the performance indicators you will use to monitor each corrective action. Some may require setting targets. You need to plan how data will be collected or ensure that the appropriate data is made available to you or whomever is assigned to update indicators and monitor results. It's good practice to incorporate your monitoring plans into your implementation action plan and distribute the plan to all parties involved.

Confirm Corrective Action(s) Are Solving the Problem

As you collect data or as it is systematically made available as planned, you need to organize, summarize, and interpret it to ensure that root causes are being tackled. The following three activities will help you to assess the effectiveness of your corrective actions:

1. Compare before and after performance indicator data.

2. Compare results to a target.

3. Confirm that a reduction in the root cause(s) has really happened because of the corrective action(s) by comparing with an area having similar problems.

Communicate Results, as Appropriate

You may be accountable for reporting the results of implementing the corrective actions. If so, you need to structure reporting to provide feedback on a timely basis. Depending on the situation, you may need to routinely update indicators, set up status meetings on a regular basis, periodically check on the status of a project, and prepare status reports.

Some of the tools that help to show results include line and bar graphs, histograms, control charts, Pareto charts, control systems, review checklists, commitment tracking reports, action plan status reports, and lessons learned lists.

Take Additional Action as Appropriate

If you're not achieving the targets you set, plan for additional action(s) as necessary.

Standardize to Prevent the Problem From Recurring

Once the data indicate the corrective actions have been successful, perform the following:

1. Create and revise work processes and standards to include corrective actions in daily work.

2. Train employees on revised processes and/or standards.

3. Establish periodic checks with assigned responsibilities to monitor corrective actions.

4. Consider areas for further application.

Report Recommended Corrective Action(s), as Appropriate

Experience has shown that the root causes of events frequently involve management issues. Therefore, you must involve management and ensure they are willing to take responsibility for corrective actions related to management issues. In this case, you will need to be prepared to present the problem, causes, and related corrective actions to obtain management concurrence.

Even if this isn't the case, you probably need to report to management to obtain approval of your recommended actions prior to their implementation by you or appropriate personnel.

If the problem is significant, you'll need to prepare a report.

Handbook Example: *Misposition of Switch 8G 176*—Develop Corrective Actions

Labeling: The labeling program should be reviewed. This review should ensure that some criteria are established and implemented for the placement of labels.

Scheduling: Dispatchers should question the plants to determine the optimal time to give switching orders. The assignment time should consider shift turnover to prevent rushing the switching order task.

Lighting: Because of the glare, looking between the lights to view the open switch was not an effective way to verify the switch position. Verification of the switch position must be reliable. The most reliable method to verify the open switch is to view the air gap. The switchman should have *repositioned himself* to view the air gap without the glare of the lights interfering.

Additionally, labeling the open/closed positions of the rotating shaft, and the engaged/disengaged positions of the coupling, would have aided in the initial proper performance of the task. These positions should be labeled.

9

Report

What Is Reporting Conclusions?

Reporting conclusions is communicating to management, involved parties/departments, and regulatory agencies, in an oral or written format, your findings and the action(s) required (or taken) to resolve the original problematic situation.

Why Is It Important to Report Conclusions?

It is important to report your conclusions for a number of reasons:

- To keep management informed of all problems identified as significant
- To provide information that may be necessary for regulatory reporting
- To keep departments involved in the problematic situation or implementation of corrective action informed
- To document your PIC process
- To provide information for PIC trending

When Do You Report Conclusions?

You typically report conclusions once you have determined the root cause(s) and have corrective action(s) to recommend for implementation—at the end of the PIC process. However, you may need to keep management or other plant departments informed throughout the PIC process. For example, once you have defined the problem, you may need to report the problem to management, your supervisor, or the person(s) who initiated the problem-solving effort. It may be necessary to gain additional help or support in determining the root cause of the problem, or to start multiple problem-solving efforts, depending on the findings you have after the first step of the PIC process.

During the implementation of the selected and approved corrective action(s), you may need to report on a regular basis the results you are getting. Most often, management wants to know if the corrective action(s) is effective and if any other problems are occurring as a result of implementing the action(s).

How Do You Report Conclusions?

When reporting conclusions, follow four steps:

1. Determine your audience.
2. Determine when you need to report.
3. Select how to report (written format, oral presentation, electronic format).
4. Prepare report/presentation.

The following are guidelines for reporting.

1. Determine Your Audience(s)

You can determine your audience based on the nature and magnitude of the problem. Ask yourself: "Who needs to see this report?" Consider:

- your supervisor and other department personnel;
- personnel and departments involved in the situation;
- management and/or corporate; and
- regulatory agencies.

Depending on your audience, you may need to follow requirements of different administrative procedures when you prepare your report.

2. Determine When You Need to Report

Once, to communicate the root cause(s) and recommended corrective action(s)? After each step of the PIC process? Periodically to update your audience on the progress you are making to solve the problem, regardless of where you are in the PIC process?

You might need to generate a simple summary report only to document your PIC efforts for yourself and your immediate supervisor. Later, if the problem recurs, you may need to report on the new problem along with the old one, and to a larger audience than your immediate supervisor. Sometimes, as a result of trending programs, you may need to merge several smaller reports into a larger report. As a result of the report review process, your report may get more interest than you initially planned, and you may even have to rewrite the report to meet needs for different or additional information. You may find that you need to meet the requirements of a different administrative procedure(s) depending on when you report your findings.

3. **Select How to Report (Written Format, Presentation Agenda)**

Written (and electronically generated) reports that document problems have many different names. Some examples are:

> significant event report
>
> problem report
>
> root cause analysis report
>
> event response team report
>
> engineer report

Each of these reports may have established content and format requirements. Select the written format based on whom you need to report to, when you need to make the report, and any applicable requirements you must adhere to. Presentations, like written reports, may need to be suitable for different levels of management within the company and possible for audiences outside of the company. In general, the purposes of management presentations are to:

- provide a forum for information exchange in a collaborative atmosphere;
- build commitment and understanding about the root cause(s) and problem-solving process you used; and
- initiate the process of management approval and implementation of proposed corrective actions.

Select an appropriate presentation agenda based on whom you need to present to, when you need to present, and any applicable administrative procedure requirements.

4. **Prepare Report and/or Presentation**

Regardless of the report format you select to use, there are eight generic guidelines for preparing reports that communicate the conclusions of a problem-solving effort. Your objective should be to make the retelling of the event and your analysis and corrective action intelligible to the technical-minded layperson. To do this, follow the guidelines below. If you need to make a management presentation, follow the guidelines in this chapter on "Presenting to Management."

Preparing a Written Report

1. Prepare an outline. Preparing an outline of the report before you begin drafting the report will help you write a clear, logical report. Outline according to the report format you will use.

2. Draft the report. The draft is your first attempt to describe the what, the how, and the why of the problem, and the action(s) you took or are recommending. It will be easier to write and edit if you keep it simple and let your sentences flow freely while drafting the report. Follow these guidelines:

   • Use short, active words and sentences, and short paragraphs.

   • Describe participants and units by title and function so that all readers can understand.

   • Provide text background on systems that are complex.

   • Omit unnecessary and irrelevant detail in text and exhibits.

   • Use drawings, schematics, maps, or photographs when a topic or system is complex or confusing to describe.

3. Edit the typed draft. By rewriting, correcting, shortening, and generally reviewing the report to the best of your ability, you can eliminate unnecessary details, and clarify unclear sentences and thereby ensure a better quality report.

4. Proofread the report. Proofreading the report will catch any format or typographical errors. Ask someone else to do the same. Check all facts, numbers, and attachments.

5. Ask your supervisor to review the draft. Your supervisor can help to ensure that the report is clear and concise. This step also helps keep your supervisor informed.

Steps 6 and 7 may be optional depending on the specific situation you are reporting.

6. Distribute a copy of the draft report for comment. By distributing the draft to departments involved in the event, you can verify both your conclusions and the accuracy of the statements in the report. To avoid anxiety about the finality of the report, clearly mark the report as a "draft" copy.

7. Incorporate comments. You will naturally want to incorporate appropriate comments received from departmental reviews. You may need to exclude some comments that suggest other issues not appropriate for the report. Be sure to keep the review comments for future reference.

8. Distribute final copy. Determine distribution and send copies to the appropriate personnel (those involved, those needing to perform actions, those necessary for approval, those who might be affected).

Format for the Significant Event Report

If you must report to management on a major event, the report should be written as a one and a half- to two-page executive summary. The following is a brief description of each section of the report.

1. Event title. This section defines the problem event. It includes the what, when, where, who, and how of the situation. First, clearly and concisely state the problem/event. Indicate the event number.

2. Initial conditions. Include at the minimum the date and time of the event occurrence, the applicable equipment condition or configuration, and prior events leading to the problem. You may include in this section any other relevant information related to the initial plant conditions at the time the event/problem occurred.

3. Event sequence. A detailed description of the event including, at a minimum, the circumstances leading to the event, method of discovery, automatic actions, operation actions, and equipment failures. **NOTE:** If a safety rule was broken, identify the rule that was broken.

4. Cause of event. Describe why the problem occurred, including the principal cause of the event, along with any contributing factors or inappropriate actions. In addition to summarizing the root cause(s) of the event/problem, you may include in this section the consequences of the event and any adverse plant effects had conditions been worse during the event.

5. Corrective actions. Describe any immediate corrective actions taken and any long-term corrective actions recommended as a result of the event. Indicate the organization that is responsible for implementation of the corrective actions.

6. Applicability to other locations. (Optional)

7. Supporting data. Include any applicable reports or forms, for example: nonconformance report, request for engineering assistance, plant change/modification, plant work order, etc. Include figures, tables, photographs, and other documents as necessary. You can attach a copy of your ECFC.

Handbook Example: *Misposition of Switch 8G 176*—Significant Event Report

1. Problem statement. On December 28, 1995, at 0700, a switchman inadvertently left closed 8G 176. The closed switch maintained the high voltage line energized, contrary to the switching order and work plan.

2. Initial condition. The substation was in a normal alignment providing the full output of the plant to the grid. A repair to the high voltage line required its removal from service. The isolation of the line was to be 8G 176 at the XYZ switch yard and 3G 273 at ABC substation.

3. Event sequence. The switchman started the switching order at 0700 on December 28, 1995. The switching order was performed as required, except for the opening of 8G 176. As the switchman approached the switch, he noticed the engaged lever pointed in the upward direction. Thinking that the switch motor was disengaged, because all the other switches are engaged in the downward direction, he placed the engage lever in the downward direction and "opened" the switch. Then he raised the engage level and locked and tags the switch.

   Contrary to the desired action he actually disengaged the motor, because the engage mechanism was enclosed and the positions are not labeled, and then went to open the switch. With the switch position also not labeled, he did not recognize his mistake.

4. Cause of event. The primary cause of the event related to *man–machine interface;* specifically, the switch and the motor engaged positions were not labeled. The labeling program is weak. Many labels appear to be missing.

   Contributing and possible causes include the following: *work organization/planning*—insufficient time was allotted for the task. The switchman started the task at 0700 and was relieved from the shift at 0730;

environmental conditions—the switchman had to view the open switch by viewing through the overhead lights. He could only see a silhouette.

5. Corrective actions.

Labeling: The labeling program should be reviewed. This review should ensure some criteria are established and implemented for the placement of labels.

Scheduling: Dispatchers should question the plants to determine the optimal time to give switching orders. The assignment time should consider shift turnover to prevent rushing the switching order task.

Lighting: The glare made looking between the lights to view the open switch an ineffective way to verify the switch position. Verification of the switch position must be reliable. The most reliable method to verify the open switch is to view the air gap. The switchman should have *repositioned himself* to view the air gap without the glare of the lights interfering.

6. Applicability to other locations. All other switch yards and substations will be notified.

7. Supporting data. See attached ECFC.

Presenting to Management

Step 1: Invite Participants

The first step is to identify and invite the participants needed for the specific purpose of the presentation. The audience should include anyone:

- whose approval is needed;
- whose understanding or acceptance is needed;
- whose help is needed;
- who might learn something useful; and
- who might be perceived as a "barrier."

Step 2: Develop and Distribute Agenda

The agenda prepares the participants for your presentation and distributes any supporting material to the audience prior to the presentation. The agenda might take the form shown below.

Sample Agenda
Management Presentation
[topic]

Introduction and Opening Remarks
Problem Statement
Explanation of Event Evaluation
Recommended Solutions
Implementation Plan
Questions and Answers
Closing Remarks
List of Attachments (supporting documentation)

Step 3: Prepare the Content for the Presentation

The contents should obviously be an expansion of the agenda and summarize all of the steps used in the process. The contents should therefore include:

1. Problem statement (including magnitude if appropriate)
2. Summary of data collection tools and persons interviewed
3. Summary of the analysis performed and root causes detected, demonstrated by visual presentation of analysis methodology
4. Description of the corrective action(s) recommended
5. Description of how the corrective action(s) will solve the present problem and prevent or minimize recurrence (trial run data, exhibit of application of solution to causal factors chart, etc.)
6. Request for approval

Step 4: Make the Presentation

During the presentation you should:

- introduce your presentation and make relevant opening remarks;
- follow your agenda and:
  a. state and explain the problem you will be presenting
  b. describe the analysis tools and techniques you used to determine the root cause(s) and clearly state your conclusions about the root cause(s)
  c. state your recommended solutions
  d. Describe your action plan for implementation
- provide a general overview of the plant equipment or system you will discuss and explain any technical terms with which the audience is not likely to be familiar;

- use direct eye contact and communicate on a personal level with your audience;
- use visual aids to support and reinforce what you say—refer to specific sections of handouts, if used, as well as using wall charts, whiteboards, or overhead transparencies;
- ask questions to check that your audience understands your key ideas or to encourage them to ask questions for clarification;
- maintain an open posture and move comfortably around the meeting room;
- speak at a rate and pitch that is appropriate for the meeting room size using clear diction and avoiding repetitive words and phrases like "you know?";
- ask for approval! and
- make a brief closing statement and thank the audience for their contributions, if appropriate.

Glossary

actions (adaptive)—Immediate actions you take to deal with the problem before thoroughly investigating the root cause(s). The goal of adaptive action is to allow you to live with the effects of the event or minimize additional damage as a result of the problem occurring

actions (corrective)—Countermeasures you take against the root or contributing causes. The goal of corrective action is to alleviate or reduce the probability that the problem will recur due to the same root cause

actions (mitigating)—Actions taken to reduce the severity of the event

actions (monitoring)—Action you take to check the effectiveness of your corrective action(s). The goal is to determine if the corrective action is not working or if the problem is recurring, hopefully due to some new root cause that was not identified earlier

barriers (control)—Administrative and physical methods/equipment used to direct a process

causal factors—A factor that shaped the outcome of the situation

causes (potential)—Conditions that appear to have caused the event, but need verification

causes (presumptive)—Causes that may be apparent at the beginning of the investigation or that emerge during the data collection process. These are hypotheses that would explain the effects of the problem, but that *needs validation*

causes (root)—The most basic reason(s) for a problem, which, if corrected, will prevent recurrence of that problem

causes (contributing)—Cause(s) that by itself would not have caused the problem but is important enough to be recognized as needing corrective action to improve the quality of the process or product. (Includes secondary and possible causes)

conditions—Circumstances pertinent to the situation that may have influenced the course of the event

event (This is the little "e" event)—action or happening that occurs during some activity

event (primary)—Action or happening that leads up to or follows the primary effect

event (secondary)—Action or happening that impacts the primary event but is not directly involved in the situation

Event (This is the big "E" event)—term used to describe the overall problem and/or result of the problem

human reliability—The likelihood of a person performing a task correctly

inappropriate actions—An undesirable event or "error"

near miss—An "Event" that almost happened or an "Event" that did happen but no one knows about. If the person involved in the near miss does not come forward, no one may ever know it occurred

potential problem—A condition that, if not corrected, could cause an event or make it worse

presumptions—Actions, conditions, or causal factors that appear logical in the sequence but cannot be proven

primary effects—Undesirable event (error/failure), the occurrence of which was critical for the occurrence of the situation being evaluated

recommendations—Suggestions for change to correct the event and prevent it from reoccurring, but that need management approval

single case boring—Evaluation of one event or problem to determine causes and corrective action

subject matter expert—Person who performs the task well and understands what/why/how each step of the task is done

A

Initial Data Gathering Forms: Personnel Statement

NAME _____   DATE OF EVENT _____

POSITION _____   TIME OF EVENT _____

DEPARTMENT_____

1. State the conditions prior to the event (this includes status of task performed or equipment used).

   _____

   _____

   _____

2. What was your work assignment prior to the event?

   _____

   _____

   _____

3. What work controls (procedures, work order, clearance, etc.) applied to your work assignment?

   _____

   _____

   _____

4. What was your first indication that a problem existed?

_____

_____

_____

5. What was your individual action as a result of the indications?

_____

_____

_____

6. What were subsequent indications and responses, including manual actions?

_____

_____

_____

7. List any noted equipment problems or inadequacies both before and after the event.

_____

_____

_____

8. Explain if there are any procedure or work instruction deficiencies associated with the event.

_____

_____

_____

9. What do you believe caused this event?

_____

_____

_____

10. What recommendations do you have to prevent reoccurrence of this event?

   _____

   _____

   _____

11. List others present or involved with this event.

   _____

   _____

   _____

12. Additional comments:

   _____

   _____

   _____

   _____

   _____

   _____

   _____

   _____

   _____

   _____

   _____

   _____

   _____

_____

_____

_____

_____

_____

_____

_____

_____

_____

_____   _____   _____
Signature   Date   Time

B

Causal Factor Category List

A causal factor shapes the outcome of a situation. There are 18 potential causal factors associated with root cause analysis. Event causal factors are generally divided into human performance problems, equipment performance problems, and external forces.

Human Performance Problems	Verbal communication
	Written procedures and documents
	Man–machine interface
	Environmental conditions
	Work schedule
	Work practices
	Work organization/planning
	Supervisory methods
	Training/qualification method
	Change management
	Resource management
	Managerial methods
Equipment Performance Problems	Design/configuration and analysis
	Equipment condition
	Environmental conditions
	Equipment specification manufacturing and construction
	Maintenance/testing
	Equipment/system operation
External Forces	Beyond the usual control of the company

Human Performance

Verbal Communication

Definition.   The spoken presentation of information. The effectiveness
of the presentation is affected by the method used to present the information.

Example.   Inadequate information exchange face-to-face, telephone.

1. Modifier—communication type
   a. Face-to-face
   b. Telephone
   c. Intercom or page
   d. Hand signal
   e. Radio/headset
   f. Other (specify)
2. Modifier—intended function
   g. Shift/job turnover
   h. Pre-job briefing
   i. Job performance
   j. Post-job follow-up
   k. Other (specify)
3. Root Cause
   a. Pre-job briefing not performed or completed
   b. Consequences of potential error not discussed before
      starting work
   c. Notification not made or required when job began, was
      interrupted, or was completed
   d. Shift turnover not performed or completed
   e. Supervisor not notified of suspected problem
   f. Pertinent information not transmitted
   g. Information sent but not understood
   h. Inaccurate message transmitted
   i. Too much unfamiliar information presented at once
   j. Information communicated too late
   k. No means of communication available
   l. Inadequate or malfunctioning communication equipment
   m. Improper use of communication equipment
   n. Not properly coordinated with change implementation
   o. Interpretable or nonstandard language used
   p. Receiver not listening to sender
   q. Much of the information provided exceeded receiver's
      needs
   r. Priorities of assigned tasks not discussed
   s. Other (specify)

Written Procedures and Documents

Definition.   The written presentation or exchange of information. The effectiveness of written communication is affected by the content of the document and the method used to present the information within the document.

Example.   Inappropriate maintenance, operating, or special test procedure/instruction, inappropriate drawing, equipment manual, technical specification.

1. Modifier—instruction type
   a. Permanent procedure
   b. Temporary procedure
   c. Informal
   d. Maintenance work request
   e. Vendor manual instruction
   f. Night orders/memos
   g. Drawings
   h. Technical specifications
   i. Clearance tagging or logs
   j. Other (specify)

2. Modifier—instruction function
   a. Normal operation
   b. Abnormal operation
   c. Emergency operation
   d. Preventive maintenance
   e. Surveillance check or functional test
   f. Calibration
   g. Contamination control
   h. Chemical control
   i. Modification implementation
   j. Other (specify)

3. Root cause—method of presentation
   a. Instruction step or information in wrong sequence
   b. Format deficiencies
   c. Instructional presentation deficiencies
   d. Informational presentation deficiencies
   e. Improper referencing or branching
   f. Unclear or complex wording or grammar
   g. Illegibility
   h. Inappropriate emphasis on step or information
   i. Deficiencies in user aids (charts, etc.)
   j. Not properly coordinated with change implementation
   k. Procedure changes not made apparent to user
   l. Other (specify)

4. Root cause—content
   a. Insufficient information to identify the correct document
   b. Technical inaccuracies
   c. Omission of relevant information
   d. Inadequate documentation provisions
   e. Not properly coordinated with change implementation
   f. Not designed for less practiced users
   g. Information is too generic (not equipment-specific)
   h. Not designed for practiced users (excessive detail)
   i. Other (specify)

Man–Machine Interface

Definition.   The design and maintenance of equipment used to communicate information from the equipment to a person or from a person to the equipment; also, the design consideration for equipment reliability.

Example.   Insufficient or incorrect label, gauge, alarm, control device.

1. Modifier—type of display/signal
   a. Labels
   b. Demarcation/mimic lines
   c. Annunciators
   d. Status lights
   e. CRT/Video
   f. Printers
   g. Recorders
   h. Meters
   i. Audible
   j. Other (specify)

2. Modifier—type of display/signal
   a. Knobs
   b. Handwheels
   c. Levers or slide switches
   d. Pushbuttons
   e. Switches
   f. Manual or auto selectors
   g. Setpoint selectors or controllers
   h. Computer entry devices
   i. Other (specify)

3. Root cause—interface design
   a. Control or display needed but absent
   b. Identification of control or display inadequate
   c. Inadequate layout design
   d. Readability inadequate

e. Manipulability inadequate
f. Accessibility inadequate
g. Accuracy of display inadequate
h. Precision of control inadequate
i. Operating range inappropriate
j. Design convention not followed
k. Inadequate audible cues
l. Not properly coordinated with change implementation
m. Uniqueness of design not made apparent or emphasized
n. Equipment reliability not adequately addressed in design
o. Nontask information distracted from use of task information
p. Other (specify)

4. Root cause—equipment condition
   a. Labels not maintained or restored
   b. Active displays not maintained or functional
   c. Controls not maintained or functional
   d. Other (specify)

Environmental Conditions

Definition.   The physical condition encounter in the work area. The physical configuration of equipment effects the accessibility of the equipment and the condition of the physical surrounding or environment can affect maintainability or aging of the component.

Example.   Inadequate lighting, work space, clothing; noise; ambient temperature.

1. Root cause
   a. Insufficient lighting
   b. Lengthy exposure to inadequate lighting
   c. Poor workplace layout
   d. Cramped conditions
   e. Untidy work area (water on floor, etc.)
   f. Too many people in area
   g. Excessive noise level
   h. Uncomfortable temperature and/or humidity
   i. Radiation in area
   j. Radiation associated with the task
   k. Respiratory protection equipment required
   l. Special industrial safety equipment required
   m. Uncomfortable amount or length of use of protective clothing
   n. Exposed hot piping, unsecured equipment, exposed shock hazard
   o. Other (specify)

Work Schedule

Definition.   Those time-related factors that contribute to the ability of the worker to perform his assigned tasks in an effective manner. Excessive overtime, rotating shift work, and working on things for extended periods of time have and influence on how well an individual will be able to perform a task.

Example.   Due to excessive overtime, a worker had insufficient time to prepare for or accomplish the task.

1. Modifier—type of problem
   a. Excessive overtime
   b. Call-in
   c. Overall schedule design

2. Modifier—general effects of schedule
   a. Unable to adjust sleep to rotating schedule
   b. Normal sleep time disrupted by schedule
   c. Not discernible

3. Root cause
   a. Required alertness/vigilance
   b. Drowsiness on the job
   c. Slowed reaction time
   d. Reduced ability to control movement precisely
   e. Reduced ability to interpret, comprehend, diagnose
   f. Reduced ability to make judgments or decisions
   g. Problems performing repetitive tasks
   h. Reduced attention span
   i. Frequent attention to nonwork subjects (daydreaming)
   j. Assigned work schedule conflicted with work preference
   k. Insufficient time to prepare for task
   l. Insufficient time allotted for task
   m. Other (specify)

Work Practices

Definition.   A method an employee routinely uses to ensure the safe and successful performance of a task. Included are the employee's practices for error detection, document use, equipment/material use, and work preparation.

Example.   Lack of self-check, failure to follow procedures.

1. Modifier—document that states the work practice
   a. Administrative procedure
   b. Job procedure
   c. Other job documents
   d. Not formally stated

2. Modifier—intended or required error detection method
   a. Self-checking
   b. Immediate check by second person
   c. Delayed check by second person
   d. Documented
   e. Direct
   f. Indirect

3. Root cause—error-detection practices
   a. Self-checking not applied to ensure correct unit or train
   b. System alignment, tagout, restoration not verified
   c. General equipment condition (temperature, pressure, etc.) not checked before starting work
   d. Self-checking not applied to ensure correct component prior to each action
   e. Self-checking not applied to ensure intended action is correct before it is performed
   f. Self-checking not applied to ensure expected response
   g. Other intended or required verification not performed

4. Root cause—document use practices
   a. Required procedures, drawings, etc., not used
   b. Documents not followed correctly
   c. Up-to-date documents not used

5. Root cause—equipment/material use practices
   a. Used tool(s) not designed for job
   b. Unauthorized material substitution
   c. Improper/nonuse of protective environmental clothing

6. Root cause—worker's preparation practices
   a. Not having needed materials, tools, or equipment at job site before starting job
   b. Not having proper information or instructions at job site before starting job

Work Organization/Planning

Definition. The work-related task. Included are the planning, scoping, and assignment of the task to be performed. How well a job is planned and organized plays an important role in getting the job completed on time and error-free.

Example. A worker was given insufficient time to prepare or to perform a task because the maintenance was not scheduled.

1. Root cause
   a. Insufficient time for worker to prepare for task
   b. Insufficient time allotted for task
   c. Duties not well distributed among personnel

    d. Too few workers assigned to task

    e. Insufficient number of trained or experienced workers assigned to task

    f. Planning not coordinated with inputs from walkdowns or task analysis

    g. Job scoping did not identify potential task interruptions or environmental stress

    h. Job scoping did not identify special circumstances/conditions

    i. Work planning not coordinated with all departments involved in task

    j. Task has repetitious subtasks

    k. Other (specify)

Supervisory Method

Definition.   A technique used to directly control work-related tasks; in particular, a method used to direct and monitor workers in the accomplishment of tasks.

Example.   Inadequate direction, supervisor interference, and over-emphasis on schedule.

1. Root cause

    a. Duties and tasks not made clear to worker

    b. Progress or status of task not adequately tracked

    c. Appropriate level of in-task supervision not determined prior to task

    d. Direct supervisory involvement in task interfered with overview role

    e. Emphasis on schedule exceeded emphasis on methods and doing a good job

    f. Job performance and self-checking standards not properly communicated

    g. Too many concurrent tasks assigned to employee

    h. Frequent job or task "shuffling"

    i. Assignment did not consider employee's need to use higher-order skills

    j. Assignment did not consider effects of employee's previous task

    k. Assignment did not consider employee's ingrained work patterns

    l. Contact with assigned personnel too infrequent to detect employee attitude changes

    m. Feedback provided on negative performance but not on positive performance

    n. Other (specify)

Training/Qualifications

Definition.   The process of presenting information on how a task is to be performed prior to the accomplishment of the task. Based on task frequency, this includes periodic refresher training to determine proficiency and actions taken to correct training deficiencies. The effectiveness of training is affected both by the method and content of the training.

Example.   Insufficient technical knowledge, lack of training, inadequate training materials, improper use of tools, insufficient practice.

1. Modifier—how was training content established?
   a. Task analysis performed
   b. No task analysis performed

2. Modifier—how long since person involved successfully performed or showed competence in task?
   a. Less than one week
   b. One week to one month
   c. Between one and six months
   d. Between six months and one year
   e. More than one year

3. Modifier—how was person involved trained for task?
   a. Classroom lecture
   b. Laboratory training
   c. Guided self-study/computer-assisted
   d. Informal on-the-job training
   e. Structured on-the-job training
   f. Part-task simulator
   g. Equipment-specific simulator
   h. Generic simulator
   i. Equipment mock-up
   j. Skill learned on previous job at another facility
   k. No training provided
   l. Other (specify)

4. Root cause—training content
   a. Generic systems or components
   b. Specific systems or components
   c. Systems or components being operated or worked on
   d. Tools or equipment used to perform task
   e. Procedures or references used to perform task
   f. Relation of task to overall plant operations
   g. Potential consequences of inappropriate actions
   h. Verification or self-checking practices

    i. Importance of quality control function
    j. Job performance standards
    k. How to work as a crew/team
    l. Demonstrating task proficiency
    m. Other (specify)

5. Root cause—training method
    a. Inadequate presentation of course materials
    b. Insufficient practice or hands-on experience
    c. Inadequate assessment of task proficiency
    d. Insufficient refresher training
    e. Absence of training objectives
    f. Task performance deficiencies not fed back into development of objectives
    g. No training provided
    h. Not properly coordinated with change implementation
    i. Inadequate simulator fidelity
    j. Other (specify)

Change Management

Definition.   The process whereby the hardware or software associated with a particular operation, technique, or system is modified.

Example.   Inappropriate modification; lack of change-related retraining, revised procedures, documents.

1. Root cause
    a. Problem identification methods did not identify need for change
    b. Change not implemented in a timely manner
    c. Inadequate resources applied to change
    d. Inadequate vendor support of change
    e. Risks and consequences associated with change not adequately reviewed or assessed
    f. System interactions not considered
    g. Personnel and department interactions not considered
    h. Effect of change on schedules not adequately addressed
    i. Change-related equipment
    j. Change-related documents not developed or revised
    k. Change-related equipment not provided or not revised
    l. Pre-job briefing/shift turnover not completed concerning change
    m. Change not identifiable during task
    n. Accuracy and effectiveness of change not verified or validated
    o. Ineffectiveness of change not acted on
    p. Other (specify)

Resource Management

Definition. The process whereby manpower and material are allocated for a particular task or objective.

Example. Unavailability of tools, information, personnel, supervision.

1. Root cause
    a. Too many administrative duties assigned to immediate supervisors
    b. Insufficient supervisory resources to provide needed supervision
    c. Insufficient manpower to support identified goal or objective
    d. Resources not provided to ensure adequate training is provided and maintained
    e. Needed changes not approved or funded
    f. Means not provided for ensuring procedures and documents are of adequate quality and up-to-date
    g. Means not provided for ensuring adequate availability of appropriate materials and tools
    h. Means not provided for ensuring adequate equipment quality, reliability, and operability
    i. Personnel selection methods did not ensure match of worker motivations and job description
    j. Job performance and professionalism standards are not adequately defined or enforced
    k. Other (specify)

Managerial Methods

Definition. Techniques used to direct, monitor, assess, modify, or exercise accountability relative to the performance of activities.

Example. Insufficient/lack of accountability, policy, goals, schedule; failure to ensure previous problem resolved; insufficient use of operating experience; lack of proper assignment of responsibility; not communicating or enforcing high standards; lack of safety awareness.

1. Root cause
    a. Goals and objectives did not address all known problem areas, such as maintenance or engineering backlogs
    b. Methods did not permit timely response to known problem(s)
    c. Methods did not ensure inclusion of all appropriate inputs in goal/objective-setting process
    d. Methods did not ensure sufficient information to support decision

   e. Risks and consequences of decisions not completely identi-
      fied or assessed
   f. Effectiveness of methods or assignments not adequately
      tracked
   g. Methods allowed approval of proposal or document without
      adequate critique
   h. Methods did not ensure inclusion of all appropriate inputs
      in scheduling process
   i. Methods did not ensure sufficient interdepartmental
      communications
   j. Talents or innovative strengths of subordinates not used
      effectively
   k. Did not communicate bases/justifications of decisions
      affecting subordinates
   l. Methods resulted in punitive response to unintentional
      actions
   m. Policy not adequately defined
   n. Policy not adequately disseminated
   o. Policy not adequately enforced
   p. Other (specify)

Equipment Performance

Design/Configuration and Analysis

Definition. The design and layout of systems or subsystems needed to
            support operations and maintenance. This includes initial
            design specifications, design calculations and analysis, ma-
            terial selection, and control of subsequent design changes.

Example.   Inappropriate layout of system or subsystem; inappropri-
            ate component orientation; component omission; errors in
            assumptions, methods, or calculations during design or es-
            tablishing operational limits; improper selection of mate-
            rials, components; operating environment not considered
            in original design.

   1. Root cause—configuration/design change
      a. Design changes not implemented in a timely fashion
      b. Design changes not compatible with as built (configuration
         at time of implementation)
      c. Design change not properly coordinated with design change
         implementation
      d. Original problem not resolved by design change
         implementation
      e. Equipment or system availability not considered in original
         design

    f. Maintainability not considered in original design or design change (maintenance/testing)

    g. Equipment not designed for the operating, seismic, or environmental conditions (e.g., temperature, humidity, chemistry, stress cycles)

2. Modifier—design analysis

    a. Misapplication or interpretation of design inputs (engineering codes and standards, regulatory requirements, licensing commitments, design basis, design criteria)

    b. Inadequate independent review

    c. Inadequate safety review

    d. Inadequate failure modes and effects analysis (FMEA)

    e. Analysis deficiency (calculations: stress, hydraulic, thermal, electrical, other)

    f. Design change prepared using inaccurate or incomplete documentation (drawings, vendor information, other)

    g. System or component configuration problem (as-built/documentation)

    h. Proven equipment design not considered (equipment maintenance history)

    i. Inadequate post-modification testing specified by engineering

    j. Inadequate or improper sequence specified for installation of multiple design changes

    k. Poor ergonomics (human factors engineering)

    l. Improper component selection

    m. Wrong operating or environmental parameters

    n. Improper material selection

    o. Unanticipated interaction of systems or components

    p. System or component functional design deficiency (logic, instrumentation, application, etc.)

    q. Inadequate supports installed

    r. Inadequate field walkdown input to design change for operability, maintainability, constructability, and testability

    s. Inadequate review of field changes/accumulative effects of all field changes

    t. Unauthorized or unreviewed modification

    u. Other (specify)

Equipment Condition

Definition.   The failure mechanism of the equipment is due to the physical condition of the equipment.

Example.   Erosion of the inside of a pipe due to steam/water droplet impingement.

1. Root cause—embrittlement, overload, stress, aging, etc.
   a. Strain—age embrittlement
   b. 500 F embrittlement
   c. Quench age embrittlement
   d. Temper embrittlement
   e. Hydrogen embrittlement
   f. Blue embrittlement
   g. Stress corrosion cracking (embrittlement)
   h. 400c–500c embrittlement
   i. Sigma-phases embrittlement
   j. Granulization
   k. Intermetallic-compound embrittlement
   l. Neutron embrittlement
   m. Compressive overload
   n. Sheer overload
   o. Tension overload
   p. Torsion overload
   q. Turbulence vibration
   r. Submerged vortices
   s. Vortex shedding vibration
   t. Vane passing pressure pulses
   v. Fluideiastic instability
   w. Unbalancing
   x. Misalignment
   y. Oil whirl vibration
   z. Mechanical interference

2. Root cause—fatigue, erosion, corrosion, etc.
   a. Torsional vibration
   b. Rotating bending fatigue
   c. Unidirectional bend/fatigue
   d. Torsional fatigue
   e. Corrosion fatigue
   f. Water droplet erosion
   g. Cavitation erosion
   h. General corrosion
   i. Erosion/corrosion
   j. Galvanic corrosion
   k. Crevice/pitting corrosion
   l. Water hammer
   m. Inadequate lubrication
   n. Interference from a moving object
   o. Misdesign load bearing structure
   p. Conductive interference
   q. Capacitive interference
   r. Inductive interference

s. Radiative interference
t. Overheating
u. Overpressurization
v. Overvoltage
w. Other (specify)

Environmental Conditions

Definition.   The condition can be attributed to the physical condition of the equipment area, or its environment, such as temperature, humidity, radiation, etc.

Example.   A worker received an electrical shock due to exposed wiring.

1. Root cause
   a. Poor layout (ventilation problems)
   b. Untidy area (water, debris on floor, etc.).
   c. Temperature
   d. Humidity
   e. High radiation in area
   f. Special industrial safety equipment
   g. Exposed hot piping, unsecured equipment, exposed shock hazard
   h. Other (specify)

Equipment Specification Manufacture and Construction

Definition.   The process that includes the manufacture and installation of equipment.

Example.   Improper heat treatment, machining, casting, on-site fabrication, installation.

1. Modifier—manufacturing/installation deficiency
   a. Company
   b. Contractor
   c. Vendor
2. Root cause—manufacturing
   a. Planning error
   b. Inappropriate manufacturing standard applied
   c. Manufacturing standard improperly applied
   d. Material deficiency
   e. Fabrication deficiency
   f. Inadequate technical requirements in component/part manufacture specification
   g. Wrong material used in fabrication

    h. Wrong sequence fabricated

    i. Defective material

    j. Lack of proper tools for fabrication

    k. Original component or part manufacturing specification used (not updated)

    l. Inappropriate service requirements

    m. Inappropriate component or system interface requirements

    n. Lack of proper tools used for installation

    o. Quality problems (workmanship, etc.)

    p. QC not called for

    q. QC not performed

    r. Inadequate QC requirements

    s. Inadequate foreign material exclusion

    t. Inadequate or incorrect spare parts

    u. Inappropriate performance requirements

    v. Not per design fabrication

    w. Other (specify)

3. Root cause—installation/construction
   a. Improper assembly
   b. Improper installation
   c. Planning error
   d. Inadequate/improper assembly or installation instructions
   e. Improper material used
   f. Other (specify)

4. Root cause—construction deficiencies
   a. Improper construction
   b. Inappropriate instructions
   c. Inadequate QA/QC
   d. Construction code improperly applied
   e. Inadequate code used
   f. Other (specify)

Maintenance/Testing

Definition. The process of ensuring that components/systems are maintained in the optimum condition and tested for operability.

Examples. Inadequate maintenance, insufficient post-maintenance testing, inadequate preventative maintenance, inadequate quality control function.

1. Modifier—type of maintenance/testing
   a. Corrective maintenance
   b. Preventive maintenance

   c. Post-maintenance testing
   d. Maintenance work request
   e. Surveillance

2. Root cause—maintenance
   a. Corrective maintenance performance did not fix problem
   b. Other problems noted during performance of maintenance activities not corrected
   c. Improper reassembly of component
   d. Inadequate preventive maintenance
   e. No preventive maintenance performed
   f. Work in proximity contributed to failure
   g. Other (specify)

3. Root cause—testing
   a. Required testing not performed
   b. Inadequate post-maintenance/modification testing
   c. Retest delayed
   d. Testing not performed as scheduled
   e. Testing not specified
   f. Test acceptance criteria not specified or clearly stated
   g. Improper test equipment
   h. Test results not reviewed for acceptability by appropriate personnel
   i. Other (specify)

4. Root cause—quality control function
   a. No quality control required
   b. Quality control not called or informed
   c. Quality control not performed
   d. Quality control requirements inadequate
   e. Inadequate foreign material exclusion
   f. Inadequate/incorrect spare parts
   g. Other (specify)

Equipment/Systems Operation

Definition.   Reflects the actual performance of the system or component when performing its intended function.

Example.   Operating parameters, changes in parameter performance.

1. Modifier—failure noted during:
   a. Startup
   b. Shutdown
   c. Normal operation
   d. Emergency operation

2. Root cause—failure was the result of:
   a. Component or system not operated within design parameters
   b. Effect of changing operating parameters not properly evaluated
   c. Operating parameters not effective—wrong operating parameters, unable to prevent the primary effect from occurring
   d. Inaccurate indication
   e. Insufficient monitoring of component
   f. Externally damaging conditions not corrected
   g. Erratic performance not noted
   h. Degraded subcomponent contribute to failure
   i. Not operated per procedure
   j. Component aging
   k. Lack of preventive maintenance
   l. Other (specify)

External Forces

Beyond the Usual Control of the Company

Definition.   Influence outside the usual control of the company.

Examples.   Storm, flood, vandalism, animals.

1. Root cause—nonhuman
   a. Hurricane
   b. Tornado
   c. Severe straight-line winds
   d. Flooding
   e. Earthquake
   f. Animal interference
   g. Indirect lightning strike
   h. Direct lightning strike
   i. Weather
   j. Other (specify)
2. Root cause—human
   a. Regulatory
   b. Sabotage
   c. Vandalism
   d. Collision
   e. Illness on the job
   f. Personal problems or distractions
   g. Other (specify)

C

Other Root Cause Analysis Tools and Techniques

Cause-and-effect diagram (also called a fishbone diagram): This shows the factors that cause a problem or event. It is particularly useful when you are able to evaluate or verify the relationship of the cause(s) and effect.

Process flowchart: This is a graphic representation of a process, showing its steps or activities in sequence. It is particularly useful for task analysis.

(See the book *Everyone's Problem Solving Handbook: Step-by-Step Solutions for Quality Improvement,* by Michael R. Kelly [Quality Resources] for further details on these and related tools.)

Fault tree analysis: This is a graphic display of an event showing each of the event's contributing factors, which "branch out." It is particularly useful when analyzing more complex problems with multiple causes.

(See the book *Root Cause Analysis: A Tool for Total Quality Management,* by P. F. Wilson, L. D. Dell, and G. F. Anderson [ASQ Quality Press] for further details on this tool.)

D

Blank PIC Forms and Worksheets

Event Statement Worksheet

Event title: _____

_____

_____

_____

Location: _____   Event #: _____

Event date: _____

Note: *Incorporate the following information, the problem (difference between the required and the actual), and the effect to create an event statement.*

Where: _____

When: _____

What: _____

Who: _____

How: _____

Paper-and-Pencil Task Analysis

STEPS	WHO	REQUIRED ACTIONS	COMPONENT	TOOLS	REMARKS/QUESTIONS

Change Analysis Worksheet

CHANGE FACTOR	DIFFERENCE/CHANGE	EFFECT	QUESTIONS TO ANSWER
WHAT (CONDITIONS, ACTIVITY, EQUIPMENT)			
WHEN (OCCURRENCE, PLANT STATUS, SCHEDULE)			
WHERE (PHYSICAL LOCATION, ENVIRONMENTAL CONDITIONS, STEP OF PROCEDURE)			
HOW (WORK PRACTICE, OMISSION, EXTRANEOUS ACTION, OUT OF SEQUENCE, POOR PROCEDURE)			
WHO (PERSONNEL INVOLVED, SUPERVISION)			

Control Barrier Analysis Worksheet

CONSEQUENCE(S)	BARRIER(S) THAT SHOULD HAVE PRECLUDED THE EVENT	BARRIER ASSESSMENT (WHY THE BARRIER(S) FAILED)
(LIST ONE AT A TIME) NEED NOT BE IN SEQUENTIAL ORDER	(IDENTIFY ALL APPLICABLE PHYSICAL AND ADMINISTRATIVE BARRIERS FOR EACH CONSEQUENCE)	(IDENTIFY IF BARRIER WAS MISSING, WEAK, OR INEFFECTIVE AND WHY)

PIC Interview Sheet		

Interview Location:

INTERVIEWEE	INTERVIEWER
Name: _____	Initials: _____
Job Title: _____	Date/Time: _____
Dept./Loc.: _____	Card/Page: _____ of _____

QUESTIONS:

PIC Observation Sheet	
Location:	
OBSERVEE (if applicable)	**OBSERVER**
Name: _____	Initials: _____
Job Title: _____	Date/Time: _____
Dept./Loc.: _____	Card/Page: _____ of _____

OBSERVATIONS:

E

Healthcare Example: Incorrect Operating Room Setup

The Event

On Monday, June 10, 1996, Mr. Doe visited his doctor to check his aching knees. During the examination, the discussion revealed that the pain in the knees had become more intense and began to affect his gait. Sometimes he even used a cane to take pressure off the knees when walking. Climbing stairs had become nearly impossible, but what really made him seek medical attention was that, at times, he was afraid the knees might buckle and he would fall. The following day, an MRI was performed. The results indicated degenerative joint disease of the left knee. The pain in the right knee appeared to be from the added stress of trying to keep the weight off the left knee. Dr. Goodman called his patient and discussed an exploratory operation and subsequent repair. The diagnosis was a torn ACL (anterior condyle ligament). Mr. Doe agreed, and the surgery was scheduled at the local hospital for the following Wednesday, June 19, 1996.

Dr. Goodman's nurse called the hospital to make the arrangements for the operation. She talked to the nurse handling the outpatient surgical booking. The "Physician's Order Sheet" would be faxed to the hospital shortly. Arrangements for the patient's preoperative evaluation were made for the following Monday.

On Monday, June 17, 1996, Mr. Doe reported to the hospital for his preoperative evaluation. A chest X-ray, an EKG, and the routine lab samples were taken. Other required forms and questionnaires were completed and he went home. The hospital admitting staff obtained the necessary insurance clearance.

With the necessary evaluations complete, the surgical schedule was reviewed on Tuesday, June 18, to determine the setups for the following day.

The patient reported to the hospital at 7:00 A.M. The operation was to begin at 8:00 A.M. As part of the admitting process, he was interviewed by the outpatient nurse. At 7:00 A.M., Mr. Doe was then taken to the operating room area, where the O.R. nurse interviewed him to complete the admission database forms. He was checked by Dr. Goodman and by the doctor administering anesthesia. He received an injection and was taken into the O.R. When Dr. Goodman entered the O.R., he identified a problem. The wrong equipment was set up for the knee surgery, and it was on the wrong side of the patient. A chondroplasty was set up to work the right knee. This procedure was to be an ACL of the left knee. The incorrect placement put the anesthesia equipment on the wrong side of the patient. The entire setup had to be redone.

The changes took approximately one hour, and the cost was an additional $1,500. The hospital was not able to recover this cost, and also did not meet the customers' (the patient and the doctor) expectations. If the patient had already been under anesthesia, this delay could have made the recovery even more difficult.

Healthcare Example:

Event Statement Worksheet

Event title: *On June 19, 1996, at 8:00 a.m., the operating room was incorrectly set up, which cost the hospital $1,500.00 and delayed the operation for approximately one hour, falling short of the hospital customers' (the patient and the doctor) expectations.*

LOCATION: *"local" hospital*   EVENT #: *96-23*

EVENT DATE: *6/19/96*

NOTE: *Incorporate the following information, the problem (difference between the required and the actual), and the effect to create an event statement.*

Where: *"Local" Hospital, Operating Room*

When: *June 19, 1996 @ 8:00 a.m.*

What: *Incorrect setup of O.R.*

Who: *O.R. staff*

How: *Inadvertent (?)*

Healthcare Example

TASK ANALYSIS – Procedure prior to Operation

STEPS	WHO	REQUIRED ACTIONS	COMPONENT	TOOLS	REMARKS/QUESTIONS
1	outpatient staff	book surgery		booking form	who, when, how, . . .
2	outpatient staff	verify booking		fax & order sheet	who, when, how, . . .
3	admitting staff	insurance clearance		routine procedure	potential problem (?)
4	outpatient staff	pre-op instructions		routine procedure	not related to setup
5	outpatient staff	pre-op evaluation		routine procedure	procedure verified?
6	hospital & Dr.	clearance from Dr.	form	fax	not related to setup
7	outpatient staff	complete "check-in"		routine procedure	procedure verified?
8	O.R. staff	complete chart		routine procedure	procedure verified?
9	Dr. & anesthesiologist	check with patient			what checked for?
10	Dr. & anesthesiologist	perform procedure			problem found

Healthcare Example

TASK ANALYSIS – Setup Operating Room for Procedure

STEPS	WHO	REQUIRED ACTIONS	COMPONENT	TOOLS	REMARKS/QUESTIONS
1	outpatient staff	book surgery		booking form	who, when, how. . . .
2	outpatient staff	verify booking		fax & order sheet	who, when, how. . . .
3	O.R. nurse	review next day procedures for setup		routine procedure	setup was incorrect for scheduled procedure
4	O.R. nurse	set up O.R.		routine procedure	same as scheduled
5	O.R. nurse	complete chart		routine procedure	procedure verified? how
6	hospital & Dr.	O.R. procedure			problem found

Healthcare Example

CHANGE ANALYSIS – Incorrect Operating Room Setup

CHANGE FACTOR	DIFFERENCE/CHANGE	EFFECT	QUESTIONS TO ANSWER
WHAT (Condition, Activity, Equipment)	"older" medical term used by doctor's nurse	booked incorrectly	why not questioned about term?
WHEN (Occurrence, Equipment Status, Schedule)			
WHERE (Physical Location, Environmental Conditions, Process Step)			
HOW (Work Practice, Omission, Extraneous Action, Out of Sequence, Poor Process)	fax not received	verbal verification identified wrong knee & did not arrest error	why booking not verified with fax when it came in?
WHO (Personnel Involved, Supervision)	nursing supervisor	background was E.R. not O.R., not familiar with surgical term	why is nonsurgical person in charge of outpatient? (mostly surgical matters)

Healthcare Example

CONTROL BARRIER ANALYSIS – Incorrect Operating Room Setup

CONSEQUENCE(S)	BARRIER(S) THAT SHOULD HAVE PRECLUDED THE EVENT	BARRIER ASSESSMENT (WHY THE BARRIER(S) FAILED)
wrong procedure scheduled	verification & interviews	standard form? policy & procedure?
wrong side identified	verification & interviews	standard form? policy & procedure?
insurance clearance on wrong procedure	routine process	how do you know what procedure to get clearance for? any checks?
possible extended time under anesthesia	Dr.'s and anesthesiologist check prior to surgery	what does Dr and anesthesiologist check prior to surgery? how?
(list one at a time—need not be in sequential order)	(identify all applicable physical and administrative barriers for each consequence)	(identify if barrier was missing, weak, or ineffective and why)

Healthcare Example

PIC INTERVIEW SHEET
Interview Location: *Outpatient manager's office*

INTERVIEWEE	INTERVIEWER
Name: *Mary Smith*	Initials: *MAA*
Job Title: *outpatient manager*	Date/Time: *June 20, 1996 8:00 a.m.*
Dept./Loc.: *local hospital*	Card/Page: *1* of *2*

QUESTIONS:

1) Who, when, and how was the surgery booked?

2) Who, when, and how was the surgery booking verified?

3) Is there anything done during the pre-op evaluation that could have identified the incorrect booking (procedure and side)?

4) Is there anything done during the admission/check-in process that could have identified the incorrect booking (procedure and side)?

5) Who completes the chart on the morning of the operation?

6) What are the procedures and policies dealing with booking/scheduling/verifying surgery?

7) What are the procedures and policies dealing with patient interviews for chart completion prior to surgery?

more . . .

Healthcare Example

PIC OBSERVATION SHEET

Location: _outpatient manager's office_

OBSERVEE (if applicable)	OBSERVER
Name: _tape of booking_	Initials: _MAA_
Job Title: _N/A_	Date/Time: _June 20, 1996 9:00 a.m._
Dept./Loc.: _N/A_	Card/Page: _1_ of _1_

OBSERVATIONS:

On this tape (made for review by Quality Department) the original booking of the procedure was recorded. The procedure called in was for a chondroplasty on the left knee. . . . The Physician's Order Sheet would be faxed later. To verify the booking, the R.N. (Jane McCall, outpatient supervisor) paraphrased the information. Dr. Goodman's office seemed to interrupt at the point where the left side was discussed, and said "right." To Jane M., this may have been taken as a correction as to "right" knee. _Check during interview._

more . . .

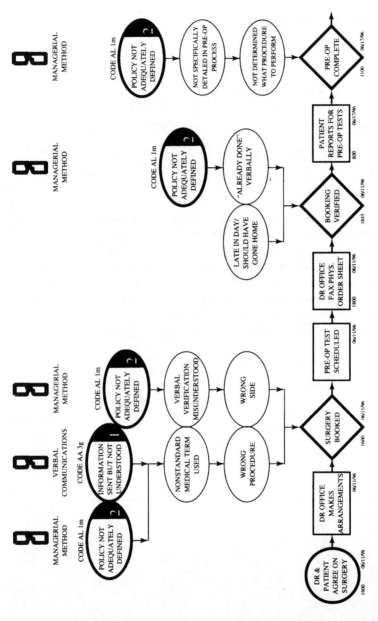

ECFC of Incorrect Operating Room Setup

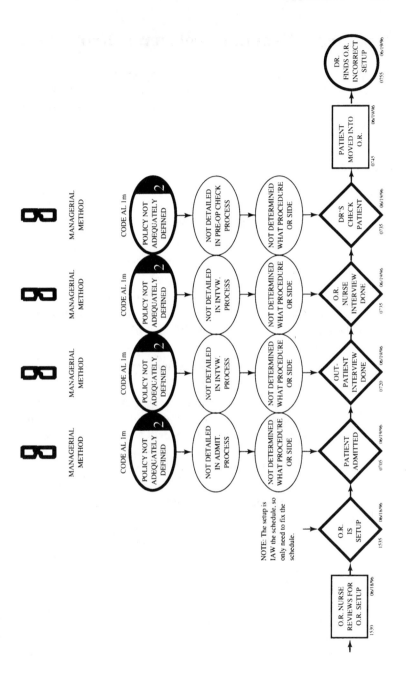

Healthcare Example: Determine Root Cause

The primary cause of the event related to *verbal communications;* specifically, the wrong terms were used when booking the surgery, and a miscommunication occurred when the verbal verification was performed.

Managerial Methods

Contributing causes include the following: Policy/process not adequately defined. Although this did not directly cause the event, these other "missteps" were failed barriers that could have arrested the error.

1) There is no policy to formalize the verbal communications that books the surgery. The noncurrent term (chondroplasty) misled the nurse booking the surgery.

2) The outpatient nurse did not yet receive the fax of the physician's order sheet; therefore, she verbally verified the booking. There is no policy that describes the verification process.

3) The pre-op process does not "require" the process performed to be verified.

4) Admitting process obtains information (resulting in the insurance clearance) from the surgery schedule. At some point in the process (perhaps when the patient does pre-op or when he is checking in for the procedure), admitting should verify the procedure with the patient.

5) As the patient checks into outpatient, the initial interview forms do not require that the procedure and location be verified.

6) As the O.R. nurse completes the patient's data forms, there is only a small block to record the procedure and location. The patient did not know the proper medical terms for the process, and the location (side) of the surgery was not checked.

7) The doctor and anesthesiologist check the "relevant areas of interest" such as vital signs, surgical release, current patient's status, etc.

Any of these steps could have arrested the initial mistake, but did not. These barriers are seldom challenged; therefore, without formal guidance, they became weak.

Healthcare Example: Develop Corrective Actions

Verbal Communications

Verbal communications are the least reliable method on which organizations rely. The booking process may take the initial information over the phone (verbal) just to record the doctor and the time, but the recording of the procedure and location should only be trusted to written communications. The process should require this information from the physician's order sheet.

Managerial Methods

The pre-op, admitting, nurses' interviews, and doctors' checks processes should be reviewed to ensure that the procedure and location are verified. The processes should document these verifications and become part of the patient's records. The documentation should lead to the next step in the patient's handling process.

Healthcare Example: Significant Event Report

1. Problem statement. On June 19, 1996, at 8:00 A.M., the operating room was incorrectly set up, which cost the hospital $1,500 and delayed the operation for approximately one hour, falling short of the hospital customers' (the patient and the doctor) expectations.

2. Initial condition. The patient was evaluated by his doctor and surgery was agreed upon to correct degenerative joint disease of the left knee.

3. Event sequence. The doctor's nurse called the hospital to make the arrangements for the operation. She booked the surgery and scheduled the pre-op. The patient reported to the hospital for his preoperative evaluation. A chest X-ray, an EKG, and the routine lab samples were taken. Other required forms and questionnaires were completed and he went home. The hospital admitting staff obtained the necessary insurance clearance. With the necessary evaluations complete, the surgical schedule was reviewed on Tuesday, June 18, to determine the setups for the following day. The O.R. was set up for the following morning.

The patient reported to the hospital at 7:00 A.M. As part of the admitting process, he was interviewed by the outpatient nurse, and then the O.R. nurse interviewed him to complete the admission database forms. He was checked by his doctor and by the doctor administering anesthesia. He was taken into the O.R. The anesthesia had just begun when Dr. Goodman entered the O.R. He identified the problem. The wrong equipment was set up for the knee surgery, and it was on the wrong side of the patient. A chondroplasty was set up to work the right knee. This procedure was to be an ACL of the left knee. The incorrect placement put the anesthesia equipment on the wrong side of the patient. The entire setup had to be redone.

4. Cause of event. The primary cause of the event related to *verbal communications;* specifically, the wrong terms were used when booking the surgery, and a miscommunication occurred when the verbal verification was performed. Contributing causes include the following:

Managerial Methods

Policy/process not adequately defined. Although, this did not directly cause the event, these other missteps were failed barriers that could have arrested the error.

1) There is no policy to formalize the verbal communications that books the surgery. The noncurrent term (chondroplasty) misled the nurse booking the surgery.

2) The outpatient nurse did not yet receive the fax of the physician's order sheet; therefore, surgery was not checked.

3) The pre-op process does not require the process to be performed be verified.

4) Admitting process obtains information (resulting in the insurance clearance) from the surgery schedule. At some point in the process (perhaps when the patient does pre-op or when he is checking in for the procedure), admitting should verify with the patient the procedure, etc.

5) As the patient checks into outpatient, the initial interview forms do not require that the procedure and location be verified.

6) As the O.R. nurse completes the patient's data forms, there is only a small block to record the procedure and location. The patient did not know the "proper" medical terms for the process and the location (side) of the surgery was not checked.

7) The doctor and anesthesiologist check the "relevant areas of interest" such as vital signs, surgical release, current patient's status, etc.

Any of these steps could have arrested the initial mistake, but did not. These barriers are seldom challenged; therefore, without formal guidance they became weak.

5. Corrective actions.

Verbal Communications

Verbal communications are the least reliable method on which organizations rely. The booking process may take the initial information over the phone (verbal) just to record the doctor and the time, but, the recording of the procedure and location should only trust written communications. The process should require this information from the physician's order sheet.

Managerial Methods

The pre-op, admitting, nurses' interviews, and doctors' checks processes should be reviewed to ensure the procedure and location be verified. The processes should document these verifications and become part of the patient's records. The documentation should lead to the next step in the patient's handling process.

6. Applicability to other locations. N/A (independent hospital)

7. Supporting data. See attached Event and Causal Factor Chart.

Other Productivity Press publications that will help you achieve your quality improvement goals.

DOE Simplified
Mark J. Anderson and Patrick J. Whitcomb
ISBN 1-56327-225-3 / 250 pages / Item DOESI-BK

SPC Simplified
Robert T. Amsden, Howard E. Butler, and Davida M. Amsden
ISBN 0-527-76340-3 / 304 pages / Item QRSPC-BK

The Basics of FMEA
Robin E. McDermott, Raymond J. Mikulak, and Michael R. Beauregard
ISBN 0-527-76320-9 / 76 pages / Item QRFMEA-BK

Mistake-Proofing for Operators: The ZQC System
Created by The Productivity Development Team
ISBN 1-56327-127-3 / 96 pages / Item ZQCOP-BK

Make No Mistake!
C. Martin Hinckley
ISBN 1-56327-227-X / 400 pages / Item MISTAKE-BK

Practical TPM
James Leflar
ISBN 1-56327-242-3 / 375 pages / Item PRTPM-BK

Process Discipline
Norman M. Edelson and Carole L. Bennett
ISBN 0-527-76345-4 / 224 pages / Item PDISC-BK

Fast Track to Waste-Free Manufacturing: Straight Talk from a Plant Manager
John W. Davis
ISBN 1-56327-212-1 / 425 pages / Item WFM-BK

Productivity Press • www.productivitypress.com
Telephone: 1-800-394-6868   Fax: 1-800-394-6286